Then There Was
No Mountain

THEN THERE WAS NO MOUNTAIN

The Parallel Odyssey of a
Mother and Daughter
through Addiction

ELLEN WATERSTON

TAYLOR TRADE PUBLISHING
Lanham • New York • Boulder • Toronto • Oxford

Published by Taylor Trade Publishing
An imprint of
The Rowman & Littlefield Publishing Group, Inc.
4501 Forbes Boulevard, Suite 200
Lanham, MD 20706

Distributed by National Book Network

Library of Congress Cataloging-in-Publication Data

Waterston, Ellen.
Then there was no mountain : the parallel odyssey of a mother and
daughter through addiction / Ellen Waterston.
p. cm.
1. Women—Montana—Drug use. 2. Mothers and daughters—Montana. 3.
Mothers—Montana—Drug use. 4. Daughters—Montana—Drug use. I. Title.
HV5824 .W6W38 2003
362 .29'0835'2—dc21
2003007322

ISBN 1-58979-046-4 (cloth : alk. paper)
ISBN 1-58979-247-5 (pbk. : alk. paper)

⊗™ The paper used in this publication meets the minimum requirements of
American National Standard for Information Sciences—Permanence of Paper
for Printed Library Materials, ANSI/NISO Z39.48-1992.

Manufactured in the United States of America.

To my children.
Thank you for choosing me.

CONTENTS

Contents

ACKNOWLEDGMENTS

My husband, David, for unflagging support; Mary Braun of the Oregon State University Press for her encouragement; Rich Wandschneider, Frank Conley, and Fishtrap for creative inspiration and a soul home; Caldera for a place to retreat to; my friend and editor, Jennifer Delahunty Britz; my friend and source of writing strength, Sarah Heekin Redfield; fellow writers of the Blue Room Group; Ursula LeGuin, for lodging herself in my heart and head; Andy Whipple for his friendship; Marian Biscay for important lessons; and Pauline Shelk for her faith and love.

PREFACE

The notion of this story finally being delivered into the hands of readers feels just like the onset of labor pains when birthing my first-born. There has been an involuntary aspect to the process of writing this book. It had a life of its own, willed itself into the world. As it got closer to publication I realized I hadn't a clue about the outcome, the impact of this story, but decided, not without great trepidation, to trust it would be a good and beneficial one. As a private person, there is much about sharing this personal account that feels risky, too exposed. As a mother, there is much about it that feels counterintuitive, anything but maternal. But the stronger sense is that honesty is healing, that telling is freeing. My hope throughout this process has been to show how I, thanks to my daughter, was able to shape difficult circumstances into something good and in turn offer my experience as a gift in hope it could inform others. Needless to say, this is my story. If my daughter were to write her version, it would be very different. I hope she does.

AUTHOR'S NOTE

According to the dictates of my New England upbringing, I married a man of similar social background. I believed I loved him. But more important was that he had preceded me in fact to the land and life of my fantasy—he had gone West to ranch.

It was something I had dreamed of since working for a summer in Montana. Driving from the airport to the ranch that first day . . . dust exploded behind the streamlined, silver Pontiac, as though the dust itself propelled us. The last light of day shellacked the red clay hills seated at the feet of the grapefruit sky. We sped like gods on and on into a landscape whose embrace I would never again want to escape.

After sixteen years of marriage, by then irrevocably in love with the land, I was forced to acknowledge my husband was an addict. He had become violent and abusive toward our three children and me. I couldn't ignore it any longer. I had already stayed beyond reason.

I was thirty-nine years old. Isabelle was ten, Nick, eight, and Sophie, five. Our evacuation from desert ranch to town in the family station wagon, belongings jammed in helter-skelter, made mockery of the pristine promise of the wide-open spaces—a promise I could not believe was broken.

Then There Was
No Mountain

ONE

Poplars

I was folding laundry with the phone cupped between my ear and shoulder. A cattle truck driver had called needing directions to our feedlot. Sophie, three, sat playing near me on the kitchen floor. Her brother, Nick, and sister, Isabelle, were at the one-room schoolhouse twelve miles down the road. Their father? No idea. At this point he was never where he said he was. And I didn't care. Every minute he was out of the house was a gift. It meant no yelling, no insults. Sophie pushed her way out the screen door. I heard it slam and saw her toddle around the corner of the house past the kitchen window, headed in the direction of the sandbox. She managed to keep her balance despite the friendly nudgings of our dogs.

"The highway number out of Biggs? Just one second." I put down the phone to search for the road atlas. "It's Highway 30. 6:00 tonight? See you then."

"Sophie?" I called, walking outside, expecting an instant response to give me a reading on her location. No answer. "Sophie!" I scanned the yard—no sign of her. I ran all the way around the house, and then back inside, through every room, despite knowing she had gone out, despite my certainty she wasn't in the house at all. Searching under the beds, behind the doors helped me postpone dealing with the possibility that loomed larger and larger: the irrigation ditch. The thought paralyzed me with fear. "Sophie!" I screamed, finally running back outside, my hand holding my heart inside my chest. The dogs joined in, ran along with me, as though it were a game. I kicked at them out of rage and fear. I looked to the left and then to the right down the ditch

that ran along the row of tall poplars that shadowed our house. "SOPHIE!" I finally got enough of a grip on myself to walk slowly along the narrow canal, looking for her in her floral sun suit, white sandals, and floating face down, her blond curls riding the gentle drift of the ditch water.

"Mam!" That was what she called me. "Here me am!" I looked around to see her sitting in water up to her chest inside the large, round metal culvert that guided the irrigation water under the dirt driveway. By some miracle the current hadn't toppled her over or swept her into the deeper section on the other side of the culvert. I sprinted to her, scrambling through the mud, snatching her up. She protested. She wanted to play in the water. She had no idea the danger she was in.

———————

What I was looking for when I searched Sophie's room before deciding to send her to Trek West I am not sure. I think I wanted to find something that would tell me my worst suspicions and fears were not true, like a notice that she got a part in the play, center forward on the team, showed great skill and thoroughness on her history report. Instead I found cigarettes, small mirrors, pipes and bowls, detention notices, tweezers with smoke-stained tips, beer bottle caps, eye drops. I turned up a stack of photographs taken two years before at the middle school eighth grade graduation or "moving up" as it was called. Sophie had won the school art award and had been recognized for her work as a peer counselor in the school's Natural Helpers Program. At the punch and cookies reception in the cafeteria that followed she hammed it up for the camera with her friends. She posed for photographs with some of her favorite teachers. She was wearing a floral spring dress. Her beauty hinted at a blossoming maturity. She directed her gaze boldly at the camera, her blond hair framing her face. She and I stood under an arch of plastic flowers set up for more formal portraits. It had the school name and the date in cut-out letters across the top. I had made two sets of the prints—one for her to share with her friends, another for the family photo album. Lucky I did, for what I found in her drawer was her set of those photographs, her face painstak-ingly cut out of each one.

Driving home from my office that afternoon the obsessive thoughts resumed. I hadn't seen Sophie in days. How many was it this time? Three? Was she all right? Was she going to school? Where was she? Three days, an eternity to me. I wanted to see her, hold her, be a mother to her. Ahead of me a car recklessly took the cor-ner, the tires squealing on the pavement. Wasn't that Sophie in the back seat? It was! I stepped on the gas. I'd catch up with them. I'd pull up alongside and say: "Hey! Hi. How are you? I miss you. When are you coming home?" Anything. A simple exchange. I was desperate for my daughter. I accelerated to match their speed. I could see Sophie between two others in the back seat. Maybe she'd be glad to see me. Maybe she would wave. Instead, she looked wildly, savagely back at me, then leaned against the driver's seat, in-clining her torso forward the way she did as a young girl to urge her ranch pony into a lope, her tiny legs kicking against his fat girth. I saw her gesture frantically at the driver with her right arm to go faster, faster, like she was wielding a riding crop. The girl next to the driver leaned out the car window and yelled obscenities at me, her hair blowing straight out from her face like she was hung upside down. The two on either side of Sophie turned and kneeled on the back seat, giving me the finger through the back window, framing Sophie's head with their gesture. Their car raced by the houses neatly lined up along the streets. I tightened my grasp on the steering wheel. Now what I wanted was to catch them, grab So-phie, seize her, wrestle her out of that car, take her home, and keep her there, keep her there until she stopped all this. My tire struck the curb. My car swerved abruptly, narrowly missing a parked car. What in God's name was I doing? Sophie turned back to look at me again, back at the enemy, the one on whom she pinned all the fear and hate she felt about anything, about everything. I let them pull away.

We'd been off the ranch, living in town about nine years at this point. I had been divorced and single parenting the same length of time. Looking back on it, I'd say by the fall of her sophomore year in high school Sophie had tasted most every drug imaginable. Marijuana and alcohol were her constant companions. She had experimented with speed and mushrooms and crank. She had been arrested as a minor in possession. It's a litany any parent of a child involved in drugs recognizes. To escape my efforts to bring her to her senses, she began "couch surfing" that fall. By November she was living in her car. Each evening I called the parents of her friends to ask if they had seen her. Sometimes they would tell me. Other times they would let her spend the night and not tell me, having, I suppose, decided their approach to raising my daughter was superior to what they perceived of mine. I made every effort to be calm and reasonable, eager to maintain the little communication these parents would permit. I hated them for aiding and abetting my child's downfall, for turning a blind eye to their children's, for cutting me out, for "dissing" me, for ignoring my existence, my right to exercise my authority over my child. By way of flimsy consolation I told myself Sophie had moved out but had *not* run away. We did, after all, make contact from time to time. It was a thin distinction that provided little warmth in my frozen condition.

Not knowing where Sophie was night after night recalled a recurring nightmare I had as a single parent. I am far away from my children. A dreadful holocaust of some kind takes place. I can't get to them. I want to be with them, to hold them. In real time, I reacted by trying to put my children in safe containers—schools, programs—so I knew where they were and, I believed, where someone, who knew what they were doing, controlled what they were experiencing.

One such container was the school I sent Sophie to her freshman year in high school, a college preparatory school in the Willamette Valley, three hours' drive over the Cascade Mountains from where we lived in Eastern Oregon. I had pushed hard for her to go there. Private education was the norm where I grew up in New England. After brief forays into independent schools, my two older children had each returned to the public system. This disappointed me. I wanted them to have the best possible education. I also wanted them far removed from contact with their father for as much of the year as possible. Since our exodus from the ranch he had thrown himself into the arms of his addictions and into the arms of young, desperate, strung-out women scarcely older than Sophie, with their hollow-eyed children in tow. So I was thrilled when Sophie agreed, at my urging, to apply to a number of boarding schools—some back East, and one in Oregon.

She decided on the Oregon school, to be closer to home. I went irresponsibly into debt to pay for this supposed superior education and to create the distance from her father I thought necessary. He was also in Eastern Oregon, an hour away. He continued to live on what had been our ranch, letting slip between his smoke-stained fingers the now empty pastures tucked beneath the sheer rimrock cliffs, the untilled farm ground now crazy with weeds, the now empty rows of feedlot pens that hop-scotched along the gravel bench above the river, and the neglected house with him shut inside, too checked out to venture out. The trick, I believed, was to engage the children in enough other activities so they wouldn't want to see him and risk being lured into his darkness.

With school out after her freshman year at the prep school, Sophie returned home in June. Despite the activities I had arranged, I later learned the highlight of her summer was not four weeks at camp in the San Juan Islands hiking and sailing, but the Volcanic Rock festival, a three-day event held in the lava fields at the foot of the Cascade Mountains. Sheriffs' white patrol cars lurched over the solidified molten-black flows, scanning the throngs of teens for beer and drugs. But the concert-goers, Sophie among them, were way ahead of the law. They had buried their stash and kegs in the woods weeks before. She drank and danced and smoked and snorted herself into oblivion, and liked it. I knew this because she indiscreetly described the details of her weekend to her friends over the phone, sitting at the head of the stairs. She must have wanted me to hear.

Life had rewarded Sophie for going to the edge. To the appreciative shouts and cheers of those more timid, she was famous for jumping, without hesitation, off a cliff into the Deschutes River twenty feet below. She nailed her Bach sonata recital with minimal practice. She repeatedly won cross-country ski races on sheer guts. This dauntless quality was evident even when she was small. I would pack lunches for the children and we would explore parts of the ranch, afterward naming the trails. There was Bambi's Trail, because we had spotted deer; Jessica's Rump for Isabelle's friend who took a tumble while we hiked; Skipping Stones where we picnicked along the river that snaked through our land on a beach of pebbles perfect for slicing across the flat, gray water. The Haunted Homestead hike led to an abandoned cabin with two poplar trees standing sentinel on either side of the collapsed front porch. Poplars are the telltale and lasting signature of homesteaders, marking the spot they chose to try to make a go of it, planting the fast-growing trees as a windbreak, for protection, for reassurance. More often than not on these walks, Sophie would let go of my hand and run ahead, her short legs propelling her precipitously close to the edge of the rimrock, to be the first to spot a falcon in its nest, or up the rickety stairs of the abandoned house to fearlessly roust out the ghosts we had conjured. Now, at sixteen, she brought her taste for the edge to experimenting with drugs and alcohol. Did she have poplars to mark the spot, so she could eventually return to herself?

In August, Sophie announced that she would not go back to the preparatory school and begged to attend the local high school. In exchange she promised the moon—piano lessons, athletics, an after-school job—all the things we had established as indicators of being engaged in life—external litmuses of health. We drew up and both signed a written contract—the first of many. But, as the ranch women used to say, they turned out to be "pie crust promises, easily made and easily broken."

It all felt hauntingly familiar. I had gone down the same tortured trail with my son who, during his sophomore and junior years in high school, modeled the exact behavior Sophie now aspired to—using and lying about it, letting down those who cared most. She began the year on track, then started to miss classes. She dropped out of all extracurricular activities. She got a job and lost it. I pulled the reins in tighter and tighter. Curfews. Counseling. Revised and re-revised contracts. The high school advisor told me to be tough, to set firm boundaries, not to keep lowering the bar of my expectations. Consequences. Terms and conditions. Grade point. She finally played what she felt was her trump card—abruptly packing all her things and moving the sixty miles to her father's. His was by now an environment of disintegration. His addictions knew no bounds. All that was left of our ranch we had lived and worked on together was an eviction notice.

Despite her deteriorated state, Sophie couldn't tolerate the nightmarish quality of her father's for long. Too proud to return home, it was then that she resorted to couch surfing, staying wherever she could find floor space, or sleeping in the car her father had, against my wishes, given her. Late one night in November I headed upstairs, the same, relentless questions rattling in my head. Where was Sophie? Was she alive? "Am I the only one who cares?" I whimpered out loud. "How could this happen? How could this happen to *me*?" There it was. The subtle strain of arrogance, of me-ness, of victimization in response to hardship. It works well, I would learn, to postpone seeing a situation for what it is and taking the appropriate action. What an extraordinary notion—that certain of us are somehow protected from bad things, don't deserve them, are too good for them, that surely some sort of magic would happen and make them go away, that bad things only happen to bad people. An indulged childhood, growing up like a hot-house plant in the protective embrace of white Anglo Saxon New England, had somehow propagated this misguided point of view in me. Who did I think I was? Thanks to Sophie, I was about to find out.

Car headlights glanced across the front of the house. I parted the curtain and saw a car pull up. A teenage girl got out and walked to the passenger side, opened the door, and, placing Sophie's arm over her shoulder, struggled to help her out of the car. Sophie leaned unsteadily into her friend's body, both nearly toppling on to the frozen ground. I came back downstairs and stood in the doorway, my arms folded in protection against the cold and the truth. Sophie vomited on the doorstep in a careless, detached way and staggered toward me. "Didn't seem like she could have made it home," the unidentified young woman said. "Is she still living here?" The question stung. I struggled to support Sophie into the house and help her to her room. "I can do it, Mam. I'm fine." Later, when I went upstairs to check on her, I found a half-clad body stretched out across the bed. Unable to get her blue jeans over her shoes, she had given up and fallen back on to her pillow. I called her name. She slurred a response: "I love you, Mam. I'll do better. I will." I helped her get her shoes off and into her pajamas. She turned on to her side and drew her favorite stuffed bear, Humphrey, to her chest. She had named him when she was five years old after the gray whale that had gotten off course, swum too far inland up the Sacramento River. The residents along the tidal river tried everything, even beating on their saucepans underwater, finally getting the lost whale turned around.

Sophie succumbed to sleep. The image of her vulnerable body, half stripped, incapable of helping herself, was too desperate for me to ignore. "How long," my friend asked after an Al-Anon meeting, "are you going to watch her circle the drain before you do something?" I was ready. Hand me the saucepan.

TWO

Decorating for Christmas

My boyfriend Stephen was helping me put the last suitcase in the trunk of the car when I heard the phone ring. "Oh my God, maybe that's her." I ran into the house.

"Yeh?" Sophie's voice challenged me on the other end of the line.

I jetted my breath out through pursed lips as I always did when I was nervous. "You said you were headed to the ranch, to your father's, but when I called Rachel's, you were at her house!"

"What the fuck? Are you checking on me? And anyway, I thought you didn't like me being out there with Dad."

I tried to remain calm. I had to lure her home. "I'm just really glad you called back. I wasn't checking on you. I was hoping to catch you to see if you would come and help decorate the Christmas tree. I miss you."

"I have a party to go to."

"Couldn't you come by before you go?" I prayed she wouldn't pick up on the urgency in my voice.

"Like when?"

"How about, oh, within the next half hour or so?"

"How long do I have to stay?"

"Well, I've made some Christmas treats. . . ."

"How *long* do I have to stay?"

In the background I could hear her friends—or so she called them. "Your mother's a bitch!" Whispers. Laughter. "Just hang up!"

"Not long. But, Sophie, do come."

"OK. OK! I'll come decorate the fucking tree! Jeesus!" She slammed down the phone.

———

The previous week, I had managed to track her down at a friend's house. She agreed to meet me for coffee. We sat across a small table from each other, cupping our warm drinks in our hands. I reached out to trace the side of her face with my palm, smooth her hair. I saw her father in the high cheekbones, myself mimicked in the arched eyebrows, the almond eyes. She looked Geisha-like because of the thick layer of ivory makeup she wore. She cried silently. She needed some new underwear, she said. She needed makeup. She was doing shitty in school. Jake didn't like her anymore. Dad was fucked up. She couldn't stand it there. He watched porn with his eighteen-year-old girlfriend. They were both crack heads. I gathered up her random statements one by one—a bouquet of longing and desperation.

"Want to come home tonight? Have some soup, a hot bath?" I offered.

She hesitated, relaxed briefly into the balm of the suggestion, then pulled her head inside the hood of her black sweatshirt and abruptly got up and left.

———

I ran out to the car. "Oh my God, Stephen. She says she's coming. She just called and she's on her way down from Rachel's." I was trembling. Stephen put his arms around me. *Yes, please,* I thought, *hold me through this.*

The houses on our street that night giddily flashed Christmas lights, birches and aspen startled to find themselves sparking red and green, gutters garlanded with tiny white lights. My neighbors moved in and out of the front and back doors of their life, oblivious to what was going on next door. Their car pulled in, the automatic garage door swallowed it up. The husband, with plugs in his ears, blew the sidewalk clear of snow and any other evidence of chaos.

I ached for the days on our High Desert ranch, winter days, days that stung my nostrils with cold, the sagebrush steely gray against the scurry of snow that whispered across the ground. I'd put the pickup in low gear to lurch driverless across the hardpan meadow while I hopped out of the cab and climbed up into the back to toss hay to the lowing ladies-in-waiting, already great with the next spring's calf. I longed for chickens flocking to handfuls of corn meal, for the easy lope of the seasons, their rhyme creating my reason for being. I was so sure I would raise my children as free verse in that environment, as part of the internal cadence of nature. I longed for the ranch, and for the life where I had begun the dream that had now turned into a nightmare.

For two winters when we lived and ranched in the High Desert I followed fur trappers with my camera, documenting what they did. I followed them not because I disapproved of what they were doing but because I respected and was curious about this ancient means of making a living. One of the trappers was an older man, seventy or so, who also delivered the mail on our rural route. He had long since given up trapping bobcats, too easy, not enough sport, despite the demand from furriers in Los Angeles for the pelts. He concentrated on coyotes because, he explained, it was an even match. He respected the animal and its intelligence. He spent the summer collecting dead rattle snakes, letting their meat ferment, and mixing a strong bait using the putrid remains. Besides dead rattle snake, the ingredients he used to create the scent were top secret, as they are among all trappers. Our dogs would set up a howl when he parked his old jeep in front of our house, such was the stench. During the winter, when the coyote's fur had set up, he would set long lines of traps covering hundreds of miles and religiously drive over the roadless distance each day to check the lines. I photographed him setting the snares.

He'd dig a hole in the ground, not too deep, and lay the cocked metal trap in it. He'd carefully cover it with small twigs and grass, and then cover it gently with the fine, dry dirt of the desert. He'd then crawl backward, away from the trap, brushing his trail away with a juniper bough. His clothes, gloves, and shoes were all soaked with the same scent he used on the trap, ensuring no telltale smell of a human would alert the coyote.

My girlfriend, Sharon, had agreed to come over to help with what I was about to do. She and Stephen were decorating the tree when Sophie walked into the house, warily, like a wild animal sniffing the surroundings for the scent of danger, of imminent attack. But I had disguised the trap too well.

The scene in my house that night fractured time. The past was present in holiday decorations crafted in kindergarten; the future, wrapped in the promise of packages and decorated with bright bows, awaiting a place beneath the undecorated tree; the present, the moment itself, a staged performance of holiday cheer, scripted, premeditated. A lie. There was an air of terrible unreality, as each did their assigned part to lure Sophie into this trap of my design, her own mother. I was playing God, cheating the normal flow of life.

The universe, many maintain, is a benevolent place. But I have learned it is also cousin to the magpie. It will pick at your blind spots. Address them or you will bleed to death. I wanted to believe the fire burning, the stockings hanging, the soup simmering, the cajoling to practice piano, to get homework done, to do chores would counterbalance all ill effect, all negative influences. I avoided dealing with danger signs by tidily packing school lunches in brown sacks with my children's names inscribed in Magic Marker and little notes inside (Have a great day! You're the best! Your Mam loves you!). I fooled myself into thinking it would be enough: clean laundry, sit-down dinner, puppies, and goldfish that survived even when Sophie replaced the tepid water with scalding hot. The tiny gold transparent bodies swam distractedly upside down, so insane was their orientation from the radical change in their environment, until I poured in ice cubes—and they righted themselves. In my myopic state, I thought I could accomplish miracles with simple gestures, could turn the tides with fresh-baked cookies. But the forces of evil, I am reluctant to conclude, hold greater sway. My guess is four to one— four times the good is needed to counter one instance of evil in the world. I learned this firsthand.

Sophie's older sister, Isabelle, had withdrawn upstairs— unwilling to play an active part in what was about to take place. She had dutifully come home for Christmas, to lend what support she could during yet another family crisis, leaving college concerns and her boyfriend behind. She must have resented it, having needed but been unable to get my attention during her high school years, so preoccupied was I with the needs of her younger siblings. Her brother, Nick, had come for the holidays from his winter job at Squaw Valley but was out with friends.

"Yeh, I'm here. So what?" Sophie wore her attitude as burdensomely as she wore her oversized clothes. "Can Rachel and Megan help?"

"No." I said.

"They're my best friends! You don't like my best friends? You *never* have liked my best friends!"

"This is a family evening."

"Fuck this. Since when are Sharon and Stephen part of the family?"

I felt certain I was going to lose her. "Sharon just dropped by. She's just here for a little while. She's leaving soon."

Sophie stuck her head out the front door and yelled to Rachel and Megan. "Fuck! See you at the party! Not long! Call me!" She held her index finger to her mouth, her thumb to her ear, signing telephone.

Every exchange between them always ended with: "Call me!" as though the umbilical cord of their destructive association would never be cut so long as that leave-taking was observed. Call me! Always keep me in your thoughts. Always remind me of who I am according to how you see me, want me to be. Be my armor. Be my strength. Remind me of our beliefs. Be my false god. Help me hate myself. Call me.

She walked toward the tree, which listed slightly in the battered red metal stand, and halfheartedly picked up decorations out of the box.

"Would you like some food?"

"No."

"You've got to eat something."

"I'll eat at the party."

"How are you, my darling?" She again dodged my embrace. I made small talk about each decoration. "Remember this one? You made it. Look, here's Nick's from second grade."

She looked around. "Where *is* Nick?"

"He's at Ben's." She seemed satisfied with that explanation. I didn't add that I had made sure he would be away, for I knew he would do whatever he could to sabotage my plan if he found out.

"Where's Isabelle?"

"Upstairs," I answered nonchalantly.

My heart was racing. I wished the box of decorations would become bottomless, that the process would never end so the next step wouldn't have to happen. But the supply ran out and as soon as it did, Sophie headed for the telephone.

"What's up?" I asked, though I knew full well.

"I'm going. Rachel's coming to get me."

I looked over at Stephen and Sharon who radioed support in their glances. I wanted more. In my fear, I wanted them to take over.

"Sophie, you're not going to Rachel's," I said weakly.

"The fuck I'm not! You said I could if I came and helped decorate the stupid-ass tree and I did!"

"You're not going to Rachel's, Sophie."

"Fuck this. Fuck you. Watch me."

"Sophie, no." I tried to sound firm, steady. "You're going to Trek West."

"No! NO! You can't do this!" She ran to the back door. But it was locked and I had the key.

THREE

Highway Motel

Stephen led Sophie to the car, which was already loaded with her belongings. Their short, anxious breaths condensed in the cold night air, panicky smoke signals. I climbed into the back seat next to her. Sharon and Stephen sat up front. Sophie knew exactly what I meant when I said Trek West. Her brother had attended the same wilderness therapy program. I had learned from what I did and did not do on behalf of Nick. Or was it the right thing, done the wrong way? I fell for the program's hype. Their implication that their program, in and of itself, would be enough to turn Nick around—I believed them. In fact, it was just a small first step. This time I knew better.

We were soon on the main highway headed over the Cascades, trading the high desert's stubborn scruff of sage, rabbit brush, and greasewood for the whispered hush of the dense evergreen forests of Western Oregon. We were on our way to the town where the Trek West Wilderness Therapy headquarters was located. The plan was to stay at a local motel that night and show up at Trek West in the morning. They knew we were coming. I had made the arrangements months before on the chance that I could, in fact, lure Sophie home and get her there.

To arm myself for carrying out the intervention, I had attended Al-Anon the previous Tuesday. As at previous meetings, I was again made bleakly aware of how many "qualifiers" I had—Al-Anon-speak for those in one's life affected by drugs or alcohol. But I clung to the notion that I was better than the others in the room, that my children were better than theirs. They had, I believed, somehow done something to create the problems in their lives, but I had not. I was startled out of my haughty reverie when the woman to my right took her turn to speak. She drew her chair in closer to the long table set up in the basement of the local church.

"I'm Susan."

"Hi Susan," we all responded in unison.

Her hair was bleach blonde, jet black at the roots. She wore clothes that dimly recalled their original colors. Her socks were disappearing into her once white LA Gear shoes. She was missing a tooth.

"It's my daughter," she said in her husky, smoker's voice. "I'm real worried. I love her so much. I would do anything." She hesitated, her voice breaking. "I pray the way I'm loving her . . . isn't just doing *more* hurt. Like you folks talk about here. I want to learn. How can I? God help me. Her Dad's a deadbeat. I'm workin' two jobs. . . . I can't believe this would happen to a child of mine. Not drugs. I've taught her right. Raised her up right. I have." She fell silent.

"Thank you, Susan," everyone chorused in solemn unison.

During the silence that followed, as we sat and waited for the next member to voluntarily speak, I could feel the feverish heat of shame climb up and over my body, like a prickly vine, spiking my cheeks with red. Who did I think I was? This woman was my sister in heartache, in hope, the shared impact of life's hard hits. Al-Anon says drugs are the great equalizer and, if we're willing to learn, the great teacher. It took Susan to show me.

Somewhere there should be a statue commemorating single mothers, the modern day Mother Courage, the twenty-first-century heroine; a statue honoring Susan seated next to me at the Al-Anon meeting in the church basement in the middle of nowhere. It should memorialize all the symptoms of trying against all the odds of adversity, in bronze, placed prominently in the town square. I could see it: a woman, with children in her lap; scattered about her feet a scrawled grocery list, stacks of bills, job applications—the shrapnel of trying to do too much for too many on not enough.

Many of the single parents I know achieve such grandeur in their approach to making life a secure and promising place, it takes my breath away. My friend Hannah is one. She had been married to a Wasco Indian. Each Friday evening she draws her children to her in a circle, a self-styled ritual they mutually created. They drum—each on one of their own making, fashioned out of dried and stretched cowhide, decorated with feathers, painted and beaded. They drum and drum until the rhythm they create mimics, then echoes, then transcends the beating of their hearts. Each takes a turn in announcing a single goal for the next week. It can be a simple goal: *Remember to brush my teeth*. Or something grander: *Get on the dance team*. None are commented on—all gently let like incense to float into the evening air. Then a meal, prepared together. When the week begins again and they return to school, to the boyfriend's embrace, to stand before the critical regard of peers—the benediction of these Fridays sustains them like nothing else. This is the ingeniousness born out of the adversity of single parenting. We must pay such excruciating attention. The net beneath us all is so very thin. And we know it. The realization freezes some of us in fear. Others it inspires.

Sophie didn't speak other than one outcry midway on the trip: "You liar! You're a liar, Mam. You betrayed me. Decorate the fucking Christmas tree?"

I felt my conviction falter. My guilt and fear wanted me to believe she was right. I *was* a liar, I had deceived her. It was so hard to hang onto the notion that what I was doing was the right thing, the best option, was *for Sophie*—that the girl talking wasn't the Sophie I relied on this extreme and unnatural effort to return to me.

"I'll never decorate another Christmas tree. You're sending me away? For Christmas? Anything but Trek West! Mam, *no*! How can you say you love me and do this?"

I fought my desire to reply, leaving her words to dance alone in the silence of the car. Had I heard it or just imagined I had? There seemed to be slight lack of conviction in what she said. Maybe she was relieved someone had taken control, was thankful for help. She soon fell asleep, her body seemingly greedy for the opportunity to rest, to heal. I looked over at her—peaceful, innocent and briefly free of the tyrannies in her life.

Father Richard Rohr, a Benedictine priest from New Mexico, came to our town a few years ago to talk about families, about love. He talked about the need for children at very specific ages to be truly regarded, beheld by those who loved them, or, as the studies he cited illustrated, actual brain development would be impaired—often permanently. Children with shaky self-esteem drown in the acned, sweaty, imperfect, hormonal waters of adolescence, he cautioned. It felt like he was talking directly to me. Had I already failed them? How could I give my children what they needed by myself? In trying to save them from the horror of life with their father, hadn't I created other horrors of equal or greater magnitude? Looking over at Sophie asleep in the car, I prayed that she would come to know how loved she was, to know her path, to celebrate life. I had prayed this way for all my children, many, many times. What I wanted to believe was that prayer alone was enough. But Derek, seated next to Susan at Al-Anon, set me straight: "It's OK to praise Allah, but tie up your camel." My camel was running free somewhere in the High Desert. Neither Sophie nor I realized it, sitting in the back of the car that night, but she was leading me to retrieve my camel as much as I was leading her to retrieve hers.

It was raining in the Willamette Valley. That's what it does there. The minute you cross the Cascades at 4,000 feet, you not only leave one watershed, you enter a whole other weather pattern, the rain clouds taking out their frustration at not being able to make it east over the Cascades by dumping an average of thirty inches a year. During winter in the mountains, that translated to as much as ten feet of snow and bitter cold—where Sophie would be headed by nightfall. Where, the program promised, matching her wits with Mother Nature's would force her to get and come clean.

Stephen and Sharon sat in silence in the front seat of the car, strangers to each other, but united in support of me and their vague understanding of our mission. Everything looked out of focus through the overworked windshield wipers. I distracted myself by thinking up an invention of a new wiper that would alternate between a bristly brush and a rubber wand, scrubbing loose the insects and grime and then wiping them away, like magic. I wanted one for my life.

We turned off the highway, pulling up in front of the first motel we spotted. Stephen went into the lobby to register—Sharon quickly locked the car door from the inside, in case Sophie was only feigning sleep. We pulled around to the back and, walking on either side of Sophie, entered the room. In their registration materials, Trek West warned of young teens trying to run under these circumstances. Their bulleted suggestions included transporting your child in a two-door car; never leaving your child alone in a room; denying your child access to the telephone, sharp objects, bottles of aspirin; or, in dire circumstances, hiring an escort service. Yes, you can order up heavy-set young men to come to your house in the night, take your child from his or her bed, deliver him or her to the program headquarters, while you, the shocked parents, follow numbly behind in your car. These suggestions and precautions reminded me I was dealing with an extreme situation. They also reminded me how much I didn't want to acknowledge it.

The cheap motel room was dominated by the smell of stale cigarette smoke, the edge of the bedside table, like charred piecrust, was fluted with cigarette burns. Tiny melted craters studded the olive green synthetic carpet. In the bathroom: four thin hand towels. We ordered a pizza. Stephen got soft drinks from the dispenser down the hall. Sophie wanted to make phone calls. No, I said. She wanted to go outside. No, I said. She fled to the bathroom and locked the door. I listened for the sound of the flushing toilet, the water into the sink. But nothing, not a sound. I ignored it at first. What was she doing? I called to her. No answer. I tried the door. Locked. I called again. No answer still.

"Sophie, are . . . are you alright in there?" Still no reply.

Suddenly, the door flung open. Sophie glared at me, her eyes red from crying, and threw herself down on the motel bed, saying nothing.

The pizza arrived. Like some illicit drug deal, the transaction was made through the partially open door, money passing from one disembodied hand to another, the security chain immediately reengaged. Sophie ate in silence, her back to us, and then fell asleep in her clothes, curled up like an unborn child. With both of us still dressed, Sharon climbed into the other bed and I next to Sophie, ready for action should there be any. Stephen negotiated his long, Scandinavian frame into a sleeping bag on the floor in front of the door. Not grandiosely, not with an attitude that would signal he deserved a medal. And considering we had been dating on weekends for only just over a year, it was a supreme gesture of support and an act of love, one I wasn't sure I remembered how to receive.

We met on a blind date. A mutual friend set us up, based on what she knew of our shared love of dancing, exploring the outdoors, travel. What Stephen soon discovered was he had enlisted in a complex family dance that was exploring wild, uncharted interior landscapes. My conclusion, before meeting him, was that the demands of single parenthood, full-time work, and single-handedly fighting the war on drugs precluded having a meaningful intimate relationship. That's how I justified keeping my heart in hiding. Companionship, physical contact, a little adult conversation—that was all I could manage. But I also felt it was my responsibility to find an appropriate father figure for my children, and sooner rather than later. I latched onto a kind and sweet man a year after my divorce; he, too, was so wounded by the demise of his marriage that our relationship consisted of staggering around in shock, holding onto one another. We didn't last, as, I believed, my emergence from the chrysalis of grieving outpaced his. I deemed him shallow, unenlightened for not embracing every form of self-actualization.

On my own once again, just before our fifth Christmas as a single-parent family, I announced to the children that we were going to bless and smudge the house, one of many loosely interpreted Native American rituals I was experimenting with. As they peered out at me through the living room window, I carefully sprinkled a thin line of tobacco and corn meal all the way around the outside edge of our small yard. I was told, and believed, no bad things would cross the line, like a cowboy's lariat around his tent at night to keep the rattlesnakes away. Back inside, I lit a tightly wrapped bundle of dried sage and beckoned them to follow me as the pungent smell of the smoldering incense filled the house.

The odor recalled spring mornings on the ranch, when the smell of dew-drenched sage blended with the gleeful abandon of the meadowlark's song. The fenced-in alley leading to the corral came right by our house, the horses bucking, twisting, and snorting as they careened into the pens for a handful of oats. It was all about morning: the dogs taking time for a slow stretch before nosing out the door, the children's father frying bacon and eggs, Willy Nelson crooning, my two oldest, then toddlers, taking turns running head-long into the bean-bag chair ordered from Sears, then tumbling out, weak with laughter, to do it again. Outraged squawks emerged from the hen house as the chickens roused themselves and flapped down off their perch. Cowboys cupped their thermoses of hot coffee, one boot heel hooked on the bumper of the pickup, as they sketched the order of the day in the dirt. It was all about day. It was all about week, month, year, like breathing out and in.

I waved the smoking sage stick into each room, like some demented conductor, and told the children this ceremony was to create a symbolic space before the hotly anticipated receiving of Christmas presents. I instructed each of them to find something of theirs to wrap up and give to the church Christmas-basket drive. As we paraded through the house my oldest, fourteen at the time, stopped, turned, and addressed me solemnly: "If you weren't my mother, I'd be scared."

I looked back at the rag-tag threesome following me, each uncertainly scanning their rooms for something to give away, being careful not to choose that stuffed animal or book or figurine, that inanimate source of security that would, by being carelessly removed, cause their fragile arches to further collapse. "*Maybe you're scared because I am your mother.*" I thought to myself.

I now think that my dating as a single mother robbed my own children of the right, the exclusive right, to their own adolescence—instead they were joined in that mix by me. It *had* to confuse and pollute their process. It took the attention of the only functioning parent they had away from them when they most needed it. Mostly they didn't like the men I saw. Stephen was no exception. But my distracted state fed their dark inclination to get away with things. They were fascinated with the sick intrigue of my having a boyfriend. So they remained silent. As they got older, what I had projected as their desire for a surrogate father became moot. They remained doggedly loyal to the resurrection of their own. The idea of *another* father sounded like work. I didn't understand that the concept of father for them didn't call up images of security and stability. It called up memories of feeling afraid, unsafe, alone, threatened, of being intentionally hurt and then being told it was funny, of being sick to their stomachs with worry and concern while lying in their beds hearing loud arguments and then chilling silences. Their deep-seated, visceral sense was that something was terribly wrong. I thought if I could just find them a father like mine had been: sweet, loving, gentle, steady—all memories of any other kind of father would go away. Clarissa Pinkola Estes, in her book *Women Who Run With the Wolves*, states that the daughters of naïve, gentle fathers are vulnerable to the predator male. That would be me. And now my children were harvesting the fruits of my vulnerability.

I was woken from my uneven sleep by the bed board in the adjoining motel room rhythmically slamming against the wall, the grunts and moans of the occupants audible. The flashing lights of the Highway Motel sign filtered into the room through the tears in the curtains, casting a fractured, garish light on my angel child, her long, golden hair splayed around her head like a halo.

FOUR

Intake

We hardly spoke as the four of us got up and gathered the few things we had brought into the motel room. I felt numb. I told myself it's the same feeling addicts have when they end one behavior but haven't a new one to replace it with. My hands shook as I took the first steps toward handing over my daughter's responsibility for her actions to her. I could think of nothing to say that wouldn't be words from a sappy country and western song. *Everything will be fine. . . . Let me fix the hurt. . . . Nothing will harm you.*

Stephen pulled up in front of the so-called headquarters for the wilderness therapy program. I peered out the window of the car at a house reincarnated as a place of business. The building, clad in clapboard and shutters, looked so normal, so everyday-ish. The houseness of it, so matter-of-fact, not in keeping with what I was about to do there—turn over my child to strangers, expose her to three weeks of trekking in the snowy Cascade Mountains at subzero temperatures as she broke trail back to herself. We got out—Stephen, Sharon, and I, each now automatically, frighteningly so—assuming our position alongside and behind Sophie. A dog across the street barked a greeting, a high school team bus rolled by filled with hooting, waving adolescents and disappeared around the corner. My hopes of being one of the parents cheering her child off to the away games disappeared with them. I never dreamed such simple pleasures would not be mine. By that evening Sophie would also be on a bus, filled with teens, headed into the mountain wilderness. It would look like a van headed for fun—young faces filling every window, gear strapped to the roof, but we all knew better.

We walked up a narrow staircase where we were greeted by the staff. They were artificially upbeat, as though this were nothing more than an Outward Bound trip, that all were here of their own voli- tion. It had the atmosphere of new students arriving the first day at a very exclusive school, meeting the faculty. Each of the adolescents was directed to leave his or her gear in the hallway and to join his or her parents in the adjacent meeting room. However, the role of the staff lined up at the stairs was not only to greet. It was also to prevent any runaway attempts. Run away! I wanted to. With Sophie. *"Let's go. Let's go. Let's get in the car and drive away—and drive and drive and drive and not stop."*

I had heard of a woman who sold everything after her divorce, hired a skipper, and took her children sailing around the world until they had all stopped grieving, each in their own way. Why was I so lacking in imagination? Once again I opted for a program to do it for me. I stayed stuck, tongue to cold metal, to what I told myself were my daily duties and obligations.

I looked at Sophie. She was masking her fear, showing no emo- tion. But maybe I had it wrong. Maybe she was curious. Maybe she was thankful someone had disarmed her, saved her from herself. Maybe she thought this was a good thing. Would it be?

Dr. Ash, the lead psychiatrist and cofounder of Trek West, intro- duced himself. He would, he explained, visit the group three times while they were out in the field and would then provide status re- ports by telephone to each parent. At the end of the three weeks the staff would meet all of us at the trailhead along the banks of the McKenzie River where we would be reunited with our children. He then introduced his staff. First, a bearded, thirty-something, muscular young man in blue jeans, wearing a wool shirt and a Peru- vian knit hat. He would be the lead counselor on the trip. He ap- parently held a degree in psychology from a university somewhere in Colorado. His female counterpart was dressed in khaki pants and was maybe forty years old. She wore a faded T-shirt that proclaimed some athletic accomplishment or other. According to Dr. Ash, she too was trained in adolescent counseling. Another eager-looking young man was introduced as the camp cook. He looked forward to putting his wilderness skills to good use, he explained. We were shown into a room with an irregular assortment of wooden chairs arranged in a circle. I gestured toward the seat next to me for Sophie. She took it initially but then moved to the far side of a floor-to-ceiling post—so I couldn't see her. It was as if she first sat down next to the one who took care of her, protected her, who she could turn to when she was afraid—but then moved away from the person who was abandoning her, turning her over to strangers, telling her that she couldn't stay at home, ripping her away from Christmas, casting her out into the cold. And those two people were one in the same—her mother, me.

Other teens arrived. Some were delivered by escort services, some by their parents, some by four sets of adults, new parental configurations as a result of remarriages or boyfriend–girlfriend relationships. Some came from as far away as Boston, Florida, New York, the balance from locations in the Northwest. A family of Mennonites sat across from me, the father in farmer's coveralls and a white shirt, his wife in a long floral skirt and prim white blouse, her hair pinned up in a bun, sitting erect on the edge of a metal folding chair. Another couple from Las Vegas sat to my left, she with long, artificial nails painted a bright pink, a ring on nearly every finger of her hand and wearing a tight-fitting white pant suit with generous swags of gold brocade that cascaded off her shoulders. He wore a blue polyester polo shirt open at the neck with the trademark gold chain, loafers, no socks, and shiny slacks that were worn at the cuffs, the back pocket tracing the outline of his wallet where the fabric was slightly worn. One boy arrived heavily sedated by the orderlies at a lock-down facility where he had been placed by his parents. It was the only way to get him to Trek West, they later explained. After being helped into a chair he slumped down, reinserting his Walkman earphones. His parents arrived shortly after. He showed no sign of recognizing them.

Some siblings came to offer support. Sophie knew about this. Though neither her older brother nor sister were present for her, she had provided that support for her brother. She had been in this very room before—witnessed the intake of her brother to the very same program. At the time it was the hardest thing I'd ever done but, I explained to Sophie, the best thing for her brother. Surely Sophie would see it that way. Surely she would never make such a mistake herself, after seeing the heartache, hearing the other parents' stories. But at age twelve all she saw was that her mother, the only constant in her life, was sending Nick away. And that must mean her mother couldn't be trusted. Sophie's sympathies were solidly with Nick. She didn't hear a word of the parents' stories that time or now, only the accounts of betrayal related by the teens—their insistence that they weren't doing anything wrong, that no one would listen to them. She folded her arms across her chest and settled deeper into the realization she had to be on guard against life, and had only herself to rely on.

I looked around the room again at the patchwork of families gathered there. A wealthy New Yorker; a recovering addict father and his former wife with her new husband; a schoolteacher and his wife who lived in northern California. Each had somehow come up with $8,000 to pay for the program. Each had separately concluded that this step, regardless of the cost, was necessary to save their child. Because insurance companies have not enlisted in the war on drugs, my solution was to further burden my already frayed line of credit—realizing, despite working full time, that it would be months before I would be able to pay off the debt. I was still paying off the cost for Nick's schooling and Trek West sojourn, Sophie's braces and private schooling, Isabelle's doctor bills and summer camp. More than once as a single mother I had blushed when I wrote the grocery check. Nightly, it seemed, after folding laundry, putting away the last of the dishes, checking that lights were out, pausing at each darkened doorway to blow a kiss in the direction of each sleeping child—I would collapse into bed and ask myself: How can I do this? My journal entries would leave off self-pitying diatribes and lapse into columns of figures: what I'd have to earn to make mortgage payments, car payments, monthly utilities, telephone, groceries, doctors, dentists, counselors, clothes. And, too, carefully scripted ways to infuse my children with the cheery belief they were part of something wonderful, bigger than our problems described, that life did have a good and kind plan for us.

To that end, every summer I wangled a trip for all of us back to New England, to the familial gathering place on Cape Cod, to the sights, sounds, and smells so familiar to my childhood. At Sophie's age, sixteen, I had a job as a babysitter for a family nearby. On weekends, I'd sail or play tennis or swim at night with my friends out into the harbor, kicking up a wake of phosphor behind us. My mother would sing and chord on the piano her annual Fourth of July tribute at the tennis club, spoofing everyone there. It always brought the house down. My father, a teacher, spent his summers reading and gardening. Other than feeling poor compared to all the other families that summered in this seaside town, my greatest source of anxiety was whether my latest crush liked me. My sincere belief was that my children, by bringing them there every summer, would breathe the oxygen of security and constancy. The chalk outlines of bad memories, miscommunications, and past hurts would be erased by long walks searching for bits of faded green, purple, and brown sea glass, in digging in the mica-streaked sands of Horse Neck Beach, trailing their hands in the lazy wake of a sail boat, laughing with grandparents, cousins, aunts, and uncles around the dining table as we wrestled the sweet meat out of the lobster claws.

A better idea would have been to move us all back East permanently, wouldn't it? Surrounded by relatives, friends? But I never saw it as an option until much later, when I felt it was too late. Like playing statue, when I spun off from my marriage and ranch life so abruptly, I froze in place. I felt utterly friendless, as though there was no one I could turn to. Unlike physical infirmity or health challenges, drug use does not inspire compassion and helpfulness from others. Drugs are the Scarlet D. Neighbors and friends do not rush to help—instead they take cover, for fear their children or loved ones will catch the disease. That felt like a personal rejection of my family, of me. I interpreted what life was handing me as evidence that I was somehow not adequate or capable as a parent or a person. I felt responsible for seeing my children through all this, yet not equal to the challenge. And there was no second phalanx of family support anywhere nearby. They were busy with their own lives 3,000 miles to the East, and, I projected, as eager to deny the reality of the situation as I. Hadn't they bought into the same ranching fantasy? They didn't want the story to end anymore than I did. "My sister? She's divorced, living on her own, raising her children," doesn't have quite the same ring as: "My sister and her husband are running 3,000 yearlings on Oregon's High Desert, living eighty miles from groceries."

I saw myself as being without help, support, or understanding except that which I bought in the form of counseling. Therapists used words like addiction, physical and verbal abuse, emotional battering, and psychological and physical trauma to describe what we had all experienced as my former husband and the children's father descended into his self-styled hell, trying, with all his might, to take us with him. Notice how I speak of him, notice how I don't speak of him. I couldn't accept what the therapist said, that such violent and distasteful words described anything I had ever come near. They didn't fit the image I had of myself, the image of the life I had signed on for. I refused to listen, couldn't watch. I slid down in my seat, covered my face to wait for the happy ending I was certain was scripted for us. But the longer I wasn't willing to look at what the children's actions were mirroring about them, about me, about our shared experience, the longer the bad part of the movie would last.

Once, one therapist I consulted looked at me from a safe distance across the room and replied: "Move away if you want the burden of committing patricide on your shoulders." "Patricide?" I asked. He slowly removed his glasses and placed them on the table between us. "If you move away, your children will not have the opportunity to know their father, to experience him for who he truly is. They will hold some image of a fantasy father. That would be very destructive, very destructive to them psychologically." *He must know*, I thought. I now think he was wrong.

By the time I did get my bearings, I believed my children were too established in Bend to move them. They had been through enough. As for myself, I was left feeling good for nothing except tracing a very small circle of existence out of sight of those who would have expected better, more of me. Moving back East permanently seemed a move bold, confident. I was neither. And there was my pride. What we sacrifice to our own premeditated fictions! I had fallen in love with the story I had invented for my life and refused to acknowledge it wasn't going to right itself. I refused to sign on for the new one unfolding before my eyes, for it wasn't pretty.

The main character in the new story believed she wasn't enough for her children—that would be me—believed it took relatives or camps or schools or programs or surrogate fathers to give Isabelle, Nick, and Sophie what they needed—but she alone could not. That feeling of disgrace, shame, of having messed up, of being tainted, was, thanks to me, as much a constant in my children's morning milk as Rice Krispies. And the way they ingested it was not only that their mother believed she wasn't good enough but, as children will, also "Our mother is showing us it is possible not to be enough. Maybe I'm not enough either."

The Erma Bombeck lists of what to take time for and do with your kids, the saccharin suggestions in parenting magazines about communicating with your children are right on. Small is good. Time together is so important. Listening. I didn't get it. I was always pulling my children back from the edge of the black hole with the aid of extreme acts of overcompensation, ideas too big for their fragile sense of safety. I was certain that if they looked into the maw of what they had experienced at the hands of their father it would consume them. Their fascination with their father's drug-induced manias and obsessions only grew in proportion to my failure to acknowledge him in the context of who they were. And I underestimated how intoxicating it is for a child to parent a parent—advising him on his latest girlfriend; consoling him when he was coming off a high, tearful, pathetic; and urging him, the father, to check in regularly so they, the children, wouldn't worry.

Meanwhile, as I layered tennis lessons on top of private schools on top of trips East, I was unwittingly robbing them of experiencing the consequences of their actions, so busy was I trying to protect them from the consequences of his, so unaware of the consequences of mine.

As a result of what Trek West did and did not accomplish for Nick, this time around I didn't fall prey to thinking this program would be the one miracle Sophie needed. Sophie had spent months developing her habit. Three weeks would barely clean out her system, nothing more. But it would give me a period of time during which my household could return to something akin to normal: no more worrying about whether Sophie would come home at night, would harm herself, would run away, would be sexually coerced or indiscriminate. Three weeks with no shouting matches, no discovery of stashes in the sofa cushions, filters missing off the sink faucets to be used for marijuana sieves. Three weeks free of the telltale smell of cigarettes, alcohol, breath mints, cheap perfume. And above all, time to absorb the fact that it's not possible to reason with a kid on drugs. Drugs lie. Drugs don't respect person, place, or thing. To begin to retrieve your child, you first have to eliminate the drugs. Three weeks to figure out what to do next.

Now that we all were seated in the circle, Dr. Ash began the intake session. He thanked us for coming and pointed out the table laden with coffee, juices, and bagels, as well as the bathrooms down the hall. As coolly, he noted that any of the young people seeking to use the bathroom would be escorted. I could feel myself flinch—the invasion of privacy, the public acknowledgment that these kids were lining up against themselves and might do something to further that cause.

It reminded me of the times in the past few months I had insisted Sophie take a urine test, to physically confirm her claims of not using. "You don't believe me!" "That's right, I don't," my reply. I whispered my reason for coming to the Immediate Care Center to the attending nurse at the counter, so the other people in the waiting room wouldn't know. Because, after all, this too would pass and I didn't want Sophie to be a marked woman. I didn't want the mothers there for their son's strained ankle from the last soccer game to label my daughter as a druggie. I surreptitiously checked the box next to "Full drug scan for all possible substances." I made the selection of "Chaperoned sampling"—indicating Sophie would not be in the bathroom alone. Her hissed protest. Our backs turned against the prying eyes of the others waiting. The tense wait in the outpatient lounge. The silent ride home. The phone call a few days later confirming what we both knew: positive for marijuana and alcohol. The argument. The addition of restrictions, earlier curfews, appointments with counselors—and the more she used, the more flagrant the disdain of everything—until, finally, she bolted to her father's and, when that didn't work out, ultimately resorted to living in the back seat of her car. "*Mam!*" she called in my dreams.

I had been coached that the insanity my children had to deal with in their father made this sort of rebellion understandable. They acted out against me *because* I was the constant in their lives. I was told they flung themselves and their rage at me to make sure I wouldn't let them down, wouldn't go away. They were searching for themselves in an environment of contradiction. The model of behavior and values I held up didn't match what their father lived every day. They couldn't sort it out. Though I understood intellectually, emotionally I couldn't accept that Sophie would use herself as revenge against her own life, would lash out against the one stable element, me. The counseling process for me proved to be much like reconstructing memory after a trauma to the brain—only I was reconstructing my heart, rendered dumb from so many beatings. I had to learn again about trust, faith. I had to learn again about my capacity to love myself. I had to place the oxygen mask over my face first. The task that lay before Sophie and me was exactly the same. I would discover that once again she would lead the way, run fearlessly to the edge of this awakening.

Toward what would prove to be the end of my marriage, I made my first of many appointments with a counselor. My husband's behavior was putting us in real danger. His humor had turned

sick, reckless. His outbursts became more frequent and violent—
particularly toward me, and for any reason he could think of: if lunch
wasn't ready on time, if a pair of boots was misplaced. Incredibly, I still
believed it was something I was doing, something that I could control
by changing myself. Nick, then a first grader, had taken to hiding in the
morning when the school bus that delivered him and his sister to the
one-room school house would pull up at the end of our long dirt
drive. His older sister would run to the bus, scattering chickens and
dogs, her tin Muppets lunch pail banging against her leg. The driver
would honk the horn for Nick. I would search high and low, eventually
waving the bus on. Minutes after I returned to the house, his small
blond head would appear from out of a closet, from behind the sofa,
from under the bed with a plucky smile. The even lines of the wet
comb still patterned his hair. He still clutched his first-grade papers and
that day's show and tell—an arrowhead he had found or a lucky stone,
a white line inscribed perfectly around its gray belly. He would nod enthusiastically as I leafed through the inventory of questions: he liked his
friends, loved his teacher, was doing well in school.

The counselor at my appointment that afternoon suggested to
me that often our children sense the need for change before we do.
Nick was standing up for that need, at his own sacrifice. He smelled
the danger, the unraveling. He was a litmus registering it was time to
get out. He just couldn't say so, couldn't get his small thoughts
around a need so big other than to stand by, stay home, guard me.
He let the school bus roll away to a place free of the madness, to a
land of gold stars and graham crackers and milk and kick ball, math
tables and spelling, puppet shows, art class, and warm hugs against
Mrs. Ross's full bosom. He had more important things on his mind.
His mother wasn't safe and she didn't know it and he did and this is
what he could do. His baby sister, Sophie, watched silently, bobbing
up and down, suspended from the middle of the doorway in her
Johnny Jump-Up.

During the intake process, each person in the circle is first
asked to state his or her name and relationship to whomever he or
she had come with. The next time around, the Trek West partici-

pants state why they thought they were there. Terse, monosyllabic answers were the norm: "I haven't a clue. Why don't you ask them, what brought me here." "My parents think I'm doin' drugs." "I ran away." The parents are then asked to give their point of view. Their daughter, one couple said, refused to dress the way they felt was appropriate, didn't keep her room neat, assaulted her mother with a hairbrush, was sleeping around. It didn't seem like enough to me to merit Trek West. It made me uneasy, panicky about what I was doing. What *was* enough? One father introduced himself as an avid sailor, a member of an exclusive East Coast yacht club, his wife as an attorney, and their son as a student at a private college preparatory boarding school where he didn't use but sold drugs. A dairy farmer and his wife had brought their son to the program because they discovered he was using drugs. They barely could mouth the words. One good thing, they reported, was that their son held down a job after school, chopping wood and doing yard work for their neighbor.

The next time around the circle, Dr. Ash asked the children to respond to their parents' version of their story. It was a unified chorus of being misunderstood or not heard, of choosing more and more destructive ways of crying out louder and louder—until the cry, the song itself, consumed them. When Dr. Ash got to the boy who chopped wood after school he asked the rail-thin young man if he used the money he earned to buy drugs, explaining to all of us that often parents see holding down a job as a sign of health, as a sign of commitment, but instead it is often a source of money to support a habit. He cautioned against work that requires almost no accountability, such as dishwashing in restaurants or . . . chopping wood. He reminded parents that often children hold up a job in place of staying on the soccer team, and that parents repeatedly fall for it. The boy raised his head for the first time, looking a bit surprised that Dr. Ash didn't know.

"I didn't need no money for no drugs," he said.

"Oh no?" asked Dr. Ash.

"Nope. Didn't. My boss gave 'em to me."

The boy's father had been sitting with his thick callused hands, for lack of a useful function, awkwardly cupping the ends of his knees, his powerful body like a giant piston at rest, ungainly in the small wooden chair. Upon hearing this, every muscle in the father's face and forearms went rigid. His hands retracted into fists at the end of his knees. His wife put her hand on his sleeve in a futile attempt to restrain his anger.

"What?" he groaned. "Amos was giving you drugs? Amos was giving my boy drugs?"

At that point he disconnected from all else that took place in the room. His wife had to answer for him. His daughters nestled up against their father's side, sensing his distress. The boy flapped in the wind, detached, not caring.

After the intake process, the parents were escorted into a separate room. The teenagers went through the bags of things they had brought along. They were issued boots, long underwear, vests, wool hats, and gloves. We were handed back in a shopping bag the things our children wouldn't need (excess clothing) or couldn't take (pocket knives, razors). The limp plastic bag felt like the lifeless carcass of Sophie, the hide of a coyote thrown over a barbed-wire fence in the desert, the shape, the container for a life, but no life in it.

While they sorted through their belongings, we were told they would hike ten miles a day, build snow caves and shelters, cook their own food. We were advised they would only be permitted to talk among themselves during supervised therapy sessions—otherwise they would write in their journals. If they tried to run away, or did not cooperate or participate, various disciplinary actions might be taken—being isolated from the others, the withdrawal of food, or other measures. During the intake I had studied the faces of this rag tag band of kids—this group of psychological orphans. My heart broke. What was it they wanted, feared, were escaping from? And why drugs?

When it came time to say good-bye, I wanted a hug from Sophie. I wanted to get a hug, as much as give one. I, the supposed adult, wanted reassurance from my child that I was doing the right thing. My need for outside approval or endorsement spoke volumes about why taking this and other right actions took longer than it should have. *I* needed a hug. I had earlier slipped Sophie the crocheted cross I always carried—given to me by an older woman friend. Sophie took it initially, but at the moment of our final goodbye, she handed it back to me. "Are you sure? I . . . I love you, Sophie." I stated shakily.

"Yah, right." She assumed the lidded, protected look I had come to know well and turned away. I walked down the steps repeating over and over to myself she was better off there than living in her car, than doing drugs.

Stephen, Sharon, and I drove back in silence. Despite their presence, I felt utterly alone. I wanted my children with me. I wanted to gather them under me like a Banty hen, the heads of my chicks peeking out playfully from under the safety of their mother's feathery breast. And a father, their father, I wanted him to be a father. I wearied of composites, of fashioning family out of found objects.

We arrived late, exhausted. We dropped Sharon off. I thanked her for her support—only dimly aware of what a supreme act of friendship it was. Stephen and I drove to my house and went to bed. He reached over and caressed my breast, his other hand moving hopefully, purposefully, down my body. I pushed him abruptly away. "First I must know: Who are you, who am I, and why?" I turned away from him, hugged my knees to my chest, and cried.

FIVE

Home Alone

Nick stopped by the next morning. "Hey, Mom! Hey, Stephen. Merry Christmas! Tonight's Christmas Eve!" He announced this with boyish glee. "Heard from Sophie? When do we get to open presents?"

I looked up at him. I couldn't see him clearly, my view so clouded by what I wished for him: not using, in college instead of working at a ski resort, more goal oriented. I was afraid to answer his questions, afraid of his reaction. I placed my coffee cup precisely in the middle of the placemat before me, ran my fingers back and forth along the edges of the napkin in my lap as though taking precise measure of the moment, as though outlining tiny parameters of battle in advance of attack. "I took Sophie to Trek West yesterday," I said flatly. And then I waited for the terrible rage I knew he would feel at being so discounted, uninformed. And worse, rage that this news of Sophie would force him to look at his own unfinished business, at his guilt by association in tacitly recruiting Sophie to drug use by his own example.

"No! That's the worst fucking thing you could ever do—to anyone. How could you?" He slammed his clenched fist against the wall, hurled one of the chairs to the floor.

Stephen watched, said nothing.

"Nick!" I cried in protest.

"What shit. . . . I can't believe you did that! And it's Christmas! Son of a bitch."

His words bounced around inside my head like pinballs, off memories of Sophie drifty and high, smoking a joint that she had received from her father with a note that read: *"Trip time? Join me. Love, Dad."* They ricocheted off recollections of Nick screaming at me, both middle fingers raised like scorpions' tails, denying he was stoned. His curses careened off images of Isabelle screaming into her pillow in an effort to muffle her hurt and helplessness.

"I did. I took her to Trek West yesterday," I repeated, as much to reconfirm the fact in my own mind.

As I picked my way through all this emotional rubble, I struggled not to feel targeted by some bad Karma. I knew feeling the victim would keep me stalled, ineffective. I had read enough books cautioning about how we name ourselves: single mother, abused, battered, emotionally crippled. I knew the toxic and crippling effect ingesting those names could have. I realized I had to look at terrible events the way Buddhism asks you to look at death: hold the possibility at every moment—not to live in fear of it, but as a reason to embrace and be fully present in the moment. It was the same quality of attention our cat brought to the Christmas ornament that dangled from a low branch of the tree. Cosmic in the simplicity of focus, in the lack of judgment—unaffected by what came before, or might come after. We were to live suspended between the dynamics of possibility, of good and evil, life and death—each aspects of the other. This is where the pinball would finally cease its nervous travel.

A friend related to me how his grandmother found herself ill-prepared for motherhood and parenting. When her firstborn arrived she would often sneak into the neighbor's backyard and study what infant clothes were hung there for their baby daughter, so she would have a better idea of what to get her own newborn. As a single parent, mothering became like this for me after I left the ranch. I would sneak looks at what I perceived to be normal households and take mental notes of external manifestations of what I presupposed guaranteed internal order. I would try these small garments of ideas on my children hoping for a predictable outcome. But it was my addiction to predictable outcome I would be forced to let go of over and again. And now? The yin—the death of the relationship with my children as I thought it would be. And the yang—the opening to whatever would take its place. Nick slammed the door hard behind him as he left. Isabelle too hastily made other plans, would be back in the morning. Stephen and I were left to spend that night, Christmas Eve, alone.

I placed their filled stockings at the fireplace instead of at the foot of their beds as they slept, as I had traditionally done all Christmases before. These traditions I had worked so hard to preserve seemed silly, foolish now. No one at home, to cook for, to take snapshots of mugging it up with their new ski hat perched on their head. All the years before, the children would awake to the overwhelming excitement and promise of Christmas morning, that promise confirmed by the weight of the surprise at their feet, the crinkling and shifting of the contents of the stocking brimming with small, heartfelt gifts and a tiny sleigh bell, always the bell. If you could hear the bell, you still believed in Christmas.

On the ranch, we would cut a juniper tree. It would fill the house with its pungent scent, delighted to find itself so honored. It must have seemed like magic to the children, living so far removed from the rest of the world, to find such abundance under the tree in the morning. Their father, a real father then, would dutifully and cheerfully assemble the miniature play kitchen from the Sears catalog. I'd lean lovingly over his shoulder, feeling the cool outline of his ear against my cheek, the coarseness of his wool work shirt, smelling the out-of-doors in his hair, and savoring the sublime happiness he and I and our three children and menagerie of animals described.

But on this Christmas morning when Nick and Isabelle came home, it was to take and leave. I had piled Sophie's presents in a corner. Isabelle packed her things to go back to college. Nick put his presents in a box. Both carried out with them the spoils of a spoiled Christmas. They let me know. I somehow felt I deserved their bad treatment, or at least it felt normal to be treated badly. I heard no sleigh bells that Christmas.

Stephen left before dawn to go back to work in the valley, his advances unanswered again. I dragged myself out of bed, wondering if I was able to give him what he wanted in a relationship and if I had any business, at this point in my life, even indulging in such speculation. I showered and set about donning my work disguise—silk blouse, pant suit, eye shadow, rouge, mascara, lipstick, hair blown dry and shaped with hot rollers, brassy gold earrings that mimicked the buckle of my belt, nylons eased onto each leg. And then what no one could see: the start of a run deftly hidden inside my black leather shoe, my bra strap held together with a safety pin, the panicked chatter inside my head. I headed to my office. In fact it was just blocks away, but psychically miles from the hold of my house. I had often, over the seven years of single parenting, debated whether a separate office was a good idea. It did allow me to maintain a professional demeanor when all hell was breaking loose at home. But it also meant that the house would be unsupervised, empty, cold, and lonely between school getting out and my getting home. When I was first single, I hired mother's helpers to fill that void. That, of course, meant I had to work longer and harder to pay them. Their task was to have cookies in the oven, to organize chores and homework, to offer a cheery hello to my threesome as they straggled home with their backpacks and PTA meeting announcements wadded in their hands. I took out ads in the newspaper: "WANTED: MOTHER'S HELPER *Mother of three seeks assistance M–F between 2:00 PM and 6:00 PM and some weekends. Some light housework. Pay negotiable depending on experience. Must have car."* It might just as well have said: Newly single mother and sole supporter of three is scared shitless and so is removing herself from the scene during the workday and wants someone to come and make it better, so that when she gets home what she has to deal with is bite size. Or: Single mother of three wants a sense of order, of well-being imposed at all costs, otherwise she will come undone. Or this: Single mother of three can't, for the life of her, make out what the right thing to do is. Help wanted.

I received responses from every strata of financial or social neediness—young single mothers willing to abandon their own children for mine; widowers, too old and frail to push a vacuum, but eager for company; Hispanics just arrived in this northern clime, speaking no

English, desperate for money. After countless interviews, I would generally settle for a student at the local community college. There was Sally,
who brought her pet rats and spent her time carefully applying makeup
on Sophie and her friends. Or Gretchen, who passionately lectured her
young charges on ethnocentrism and the destruction of the environment. And Patty, who earnestly tried to teach the children how to
meditate, sitting crossed legged with them on the kitchen floor, their
small hands, in imitation of hers, resting on their knees, eyes shut,
mouthing "Om" in unison. To help cover the cost of these mother's
helpers, I rented a room in the basement to out-of-town student ath-
letes wanting to train with the local ski racing program. It made perfect
sense to me. The house, I told myself, was not a lonely place. It was
bustling, cheerful. The children's needs were being met and the good
outweighed the bad. This is what I told myself.

Once Isabelle left for college, Nick was a high school senior, and
Sophie was in seventh grade, I felt a mother's helper was a luxury I
could no longer afford. I calculated that with Sophie's Monday and
Thursday activities, she wouldn't be left alone too much, wouldn't
feel abandoned. I would race out of my office, run to the car, drive
home, honk the horn and wait for her to come out the front door
with sheet music or riding crop—and then I would sleep in the car
while I waited for her at her lesson—like some drunk passed out on
the steering wheel. Quality time together? The schedule quickly re-
solved itself around her not coming home after school on Tuesdays,
Wednesdays, or Fridays. And on days she had after-school activities
she increasingly would hang out somewhere other than home until
it was time for me to pick her up. She would call from a friend's and
say she was doing homework there.

"Who is there?"

"Just me and Julie."

"Are her parents home?"

"No. But they will be."

Empty houses, parents working, families whose values were unknown to me—just like the grandmother scanning the clothesline
for clues, when I went to pick up Sophie I would scan their living

rooms, scrutinize the small talk, the sincerity of the smile, the color of curtains, the choice in magazines, the photos on the refrigerator for signs. Or I would call and speak to a parent about what their expectations were of their child—matching my curfews against theirs, my requirement that an adult be present if Sophie spent the night. They always agreed with me. Despite the smooth exterior of my plan, there were deep crevasses underneath—deep fissures carved by my reluctance to take charge, to assume responsibility actively, not just intellectually, to advocate for my child—crevasses that Sophie fell into in her choice of friends, the activities she kept and those she discarded, the false manifestations of support she allied with and the sincere ones she discounted.

On that Monday when I walked into my office, I had only three weeks. Three weeks to fully realize, truly accept that the wilderness program wouldn't be enough to turn Sophie around—and all the associated implications of that realization: sending Sophie away for an undetermined length of time, where, the cost to do that, Isabelle's and Nick's reactions. Three weeks to learn to show up, be present, and do the right thing for my child. I could feel myself succumbing to the easy ether of false hopes that Trek West would deliver me a fixed kid. But no. I knew better. It had only taken Nick two weeks to return to drug use after returning. His peer group sat and waited on the fence like vultures until Nick's resolve started to weaken. It is a threat to their demented order of things when one of their tribe tries to change. Out of a sinister unconsciousness they do whatever they can to reclaim the deserter. Their power is enormous. Making new friends is hard. After only three weeks, the muscles to resist drugs and drug-using friends have barely been flexed. Old habits can seem like a familiar and comfortable slipper, more like home than new rules and expectations. If ever, and I knew this now, this was the time to abandon fantasies of instant recovery, of the ability of a single, working parent to be able to provide a recovering child with the round-the-clock support needed.

Between researching various programs, I had to field calls from my business clients as evenly as I could. I squeezed this crisis, as I had others before it, between professional obligations. Too often our family needs got short shrift in deference to earning a living, were dealt with in the margins of late afternoons, evenings, and weekends. At my office I answered the telephone in a calm voice, let the client know their public relations plan would be forthcoming in two days. I had, I assured them, provided the information to the target publications we had discussed, the articles they had requested were being researched, and everything was under control. The things on the top of my desk were arranged to perfection—TO DO file, individual client files, a calendar of appointments, payables, receivables. A potted palm stood in the corner next to a small conference table with my business cards displayed in a plastic holder in the middle. Above the table, college degrees and state commission appointments in neat black frames climbed like a vine of accomplishment evenly up the wall. My children weren't fooled. They had experienced my disconnection, fear, and unavailability firsthand—and no doubt saw my office as a monument to all three.

I got hold of a copy of *The Woodbury Report*, a listing of programs for troubled adolescents in the West, put together by a man named Lon Woodbury. He had previously been on the staff of a residential program and had gone on to consult. He included a brief description about each one—size, philosophy, setting. Those not included in his directory I deemed conspicuous by their absence. In my search I was overwhelmed by what was nothing less than a proliferation of "emotional growth" programs across the United States within the last five to ten years, each promising to help young adults with drug and behavioral issues. Emotional growth was a growth industry. Drug use meant job security for those involved. The directory included programs that were militaristic or small family models. Some were located on fancy campuses, others in the wilderness, in the tropics, or in hospital-like settings. Some even offered a warranty for God's sake, a guarantee that your child would be delivered back to you drug-free, cured of any addictions. The credentials for operating such programs were loosely defined. Standards for assessing their efficacy and the emotional and physical safety of participants seemed lacking. The costs ranged from $7,000 per month down to $2,000.

I called a few of the higher priced ones to request their information and to find out why they were so expensive. They rattled off statistics relating to student-to-staff ratio, facilities, high school equivalency, security measures, caliber of psychiatric staff. I called the state program representatives who explained the elaborate and time-consuming referral process required. They also indicated, as the only option that offered any insurance relief, that the waiting list was very long. I then called the lower priced programs. Amazing how quickly I came to see $2,000 per month as "lower priced." Generally speaking, these programs were either brand new, and therefore had no track record and were eager to build "clientele," or they were operated outside of the United States—in the American Samoas or Jamaica or Europe—where labor costs were low and, presumably, the tax and income structure was different. They, of course, explained their location as a form of insurance that my child would remain well removed from bad influences for the needed amount of time. In response to: "Hello, I want a program for Sophie, my daughter." I would hear: "Our approach in dealing with these kids is . . ." "No." I thought. "*You don't seem to understand. I am not calling about these kids, all kids, but an individual. A unique, magical, bright, funny, quirky, talented, athletic, hurting girl child.*"

By the end of the first week the mail started to arrive. Lots of it. North Star, New Leaf, Swift River, Three Creeks, TEEN HELP, CEDU. I must have heard from fifty different programs and I had only inquired in three western states. Some sent videos with tours of dormitory rooms, the campus, the attentive counselors, and smiling, well-adjusted looking kids. Many enclosed expensive, four-color, glossy information packets. In one program Sophie would not be allowed any outside contact for the first month, depending on her "attitude," which, when I called for clarification, they weren't able to define, not to my satisfaction. Others stated that there would be no parental visits for at least twelve weeks. Some removed all access to music and telephones. Others measured the participants' success according to a one-size-fits-all, single set of benchmarks applied to each in the program. Some were single sex, others co-ed. Almost all promised some means of continuing with a high school education. Where was Sophie in any of this? What of these measures were proven, were necessary, and would honor who Sophie was?

Back at home, alone that night, I put away the last remnants of our Christmas, dismantling what had been installed in hope, out of a wish for things to get better. The Christmas, the birth, the promise, the miracle. I needed one for Sophie. I needed one for Isabelle, for Nick. I needed one for myself. In conferring with my brother, he said it was time to let life bounce me back, instead of trying so hard to manufacture the bounce for all of us. *Life to bounce me back.* The faith and trust implicit in that statement was something I could dimly recall having had. Faith and trust? Which life is this? My brother's matter-of-fact assumption that life could provide such bouncing back, and that I had forgotten, made me profoundly sad. Were we from the same family? Was I capable of remembering? I watched my neighbors out the window, actually engaged by the patterns of their existence—like they had meaning—retrieving the newspaper from off the doorstep, carefully sorting bottles from plastic jugs on curbside recycling day. My days were like my dreams in which the house I lived in was crumbling around me, water flooding in through the doors and windows, the dogs and horses from the ranch stampeding by, making no sound, eyes rolled white back in their sockets, and my children nowhere to be found. Detached and removed, feeling nothing, I watched myself go through the motions of each day. Gravity no longer seemed to operate in my world. Everything was floating, loose. Walls and floors didn't exist. When I thought I had smiled, in fact my face had not changed expression; no one answered the number I dialed for help; my friends were no one I knew. Like an outsider looking in, I observed myself valiantly but vainly trying to impose a sense of order, to ascribe rehabilitated meanings to a scenario that spoke only of meaninglessness. Who was I kidding? Didn't I know I was a pawn in this game, in this chaos, this maelstrom, spinning on my back like a spring fly?

What is interesting about the phrase "hit bottom" is it implies you have stopped falling. That something has ended. When I began to emerge from the debilitating depression that had taken hold of me in the midst of all this, when I got to that bottom place, I was almost giddy with relief that there *was* a bottom, that the falling part wasn't going to last forever. I was able to laugh at how similar really wonderful occurrences and really horrible ones were for me. They both effectively brought me to my knees, to supplication, to prayer. What I found of me at the bottom was crystalline, purified, refined, tailings gone. It was surrender. It was awe. It was the end of chatter. It was beyond pretense and trying and wishing. Maybe prayer, true prayer, is not requesting, wishing—a position of weakness, really—but stating, even demanding. Many had suggested I medicate my way through all this. I am so glad I didn't listen to them. I wouldn't have missed it. This purging through melancholia is not to be numbed or avoided. Supplication. Prayer. I had lost my way and was ready to appeal to Someone who reputedly could help. I surrendered to the task of finding a program for Sophie and to the realization that I couldn't do it by myself. I acknowledged I didn't know where help would come from. I acted on faith, not out of control.

Two educational consultants familiar with emotional growth programs in the West had been recommended to me; the one in Seattle was considered better than the other. I promised myself whomever answered in person was the consultant I would use. I had received the field report from Trek West reporting that Sophie was participating, had a good attitude. They were camped in deep snow, but the storm system had lifted. Their Christmas, Dr. Ash reported, had been a sharing of personal stories. They had decorated a small evergreen near the campsite with sausage skins tied together to make a garland. He described Christmas morning as sunny and stunningly beautiful at their snowy perch high in the Cascades. He'd see me in two weeks. I dialed the Seattle number and got the answering machine. I dialed the second number, the consultant in Idaho, and she answered. We were in business.

I explained my circumstances, time frame, budgetary limitations. She detailed what she would and wouldn't provide for her $500 fee. She would, she explained, review the material I sent, the content of our interviews, confer with me three times on the phone, then recommend three options. They would all be out of state, she told me, to reduce the possibility of any of Sophie's friends or her father coming and getting her or of Sophie running away. She would not, she emphasized, endorse any single one to protect herself from any liability. The final decision would be mine. She would provide me with names and telephone numbers of key contacts at each facility and of families whose children had gone through the programs. I could feel my fledgling faith falter. Sure . . . who couldn't pull three out of a hat?

One week left. At my office the next morning, I called Trek West to tell them I was considering a long-term program for Sophie. They told me to notify them as soon as I knew, because Sophie was, in good faith, basing the plan and contract they required her to draw up on the assumption she was coming home. I felt the chill hand of fear seize my throat. How could I do this? How could I tear her away again? Was I kidnapping her, stealing from her the right to design her own life, or was I pulling her out of the way of an oncoming train? The Idaho consultant called me back, her second conference call of the three I had paid for. She had just heard that a former associate at a respected program in Montana had left to start a new, smaller program called Northern Lights, for girls only. The woman, she said, had the reputation of being effective in the various programs she had worked in. She had returned to her hometown in Montana with her husband and young son to reclaim the family ranch. She was taking in no more than six girls. The consultant had already given me the contact information at the other two programs she recommended, one in Jamaica and one in Idaho, and now added this one. She also gave me names and telephone numbers of families willing to talk about their child's experience in each of the programs. I quickly ruled out the Jamaica option as too far away for my own comfort level.

The second option, Marks Creek in Idaho, relied exclusively on a tiered step program. The students wore uniforms. Life was very regimented. There were as many as thirty to sixty kids in treatment at a time. The program had an excellent track record. I called a family in Sacramento who had sent their son there. For their son the militaristic and regimented approach was exactly right: clear boundaries, clear expectations. They also felt the support given the parent was important. They had gone through the same step program as their child in seminars organized by the program in their area. I finally got a call back from the actual director. In questioning him about the approach and philosophy, he alluded that the goal was to replace the kids' "stinking thinking" with a positive outlook. The staff weren't counselors per se, he explained, but all were required to go through the program's training. In pushing for more details I asked what the training included. "Motivational tapes and how to use them to help the kids form a different image of themselves. Like Zig Ziglar tapes. Like that." If my daughter was going to have her negative thinking surgically removed and replaced with some other, Zig Ziglar wouldn't be my pick. I realized to accept this program's approach I would have to sign over Sophie, knowing that parts of her that made her unique and wonderful might accidentally get thrown out along with what wasn't serving her well.

I picked up the phone and called the Montana number. "Hello, is Fay Clarno there, please," I asked.

"This is Fay."

"I'm calling to talk to you about, about the possibility of my daughter attending your program."

She laughed a ready, full laugh. "Don't know as I'd call it a program. I'm only just getting started. But the approach I'm sure of. The program—well, if it ever becomes *that* I'm not sure it will be listening to the needs of each girl."

We talked at length. Music?

"I want to hear what they're listening to. Talk with them about what it means to them, what they get from it."

Telephone contact?

"At first I'll monitor the calls along with letters and packages. Eventually that won't be necessary."

High school?

"She'd be home schooled first, and then, when she's ready, she'll mainstream into the local high school. But you should know, my focus early-on isn't high school credits, it's helping her to stop hurting."

Staff?

"I have a counselor and a teacher. Also, two young women who were enrolled as participants in the last program I worked with have circled back to help me get this started."

Her training?

"Masters in social work."

How long did she think Sophie would have to stay?

"A year, maybe less. Hard to say without knowing her. These kids will right themselves, given the chance, but it takes time. They develop their drug habit over a long period of time. Takes a while to unravel that and get to the real work of why they turned to drugs in the first place."

The facility?

Fay laughed her full, rich laugh again. "Kind of like the program. I'm back on the family ranch that was neglected for a long time after my father died. I'll be moving a three-story house on to the property for the girls, but here at the start, it's pretty basic."

What did she mean by "basic"?

"Well, I'll be housing the girls at my mother's until things get situated and the house gets moved."

The cost?

"Two thousand a month, plus a $1,500 deposit."

My greatest concern, beyond how in the world to pay for either option, beyond the uncertainty about the living conditions, beyond my concerns about it being a start-up, was how dependent the success or failure of the program was on Fay. The others had a system and a trained staff. They didn't depend on just one person. What if she got sick? How could one person be available to six girls plus the demands of her family and a ranch? It wasn't possible. It simply wasn't possible. As I left the office on Thursday, I had decided, Zig Ziglar notwithstanding, Marks Creek in Idaho was the one. Stephen would arrive on Friday and we would head to the out-take from Trek West Saturday morning. Time had run out, a decision was necessary, and I had made one.

But at home that night, the choice of Marks Creek didn't sit well with me. I agonized that the perfect program was probably the one I hadn't called or inquired about. Maybe this consultant hadn't pointed me in the right direction. Where was my faith and trust now? One of the references I had for Fay was a family in Connecticut. Their daughter had been in the program Fay worked in before starting her own and was now one of the helpers on Fay's staff. Despite the fact it was 10:00 P.M. back East, I dialed the number. A man answered. I explained the reason for my call and apologized for the late hour. "No bother at all. I would talk about how wonderful Fay is at any hour of the day or night," he exclaimed. "And I know my wife would second that motion, but she's away visiting her sister." He went on to describe Fay's amazing way of relating to teenagers. "She has an instinct that goes beyond formal training," he stated. "It's hard to explain, but she is truly gifted. She seems to have a sixth sense when it comes to understanding adolescent girls."

"And the staff, the facility?" I asked.

"At the start, some of that will require a leap of faith on your part," he replied cautiously. "It's a work in progress." We spoke further about his own daughter, and how critical Fay had been in helping her "right herself." I hung up and sat by the phone in silence. In reflecting on what I had just heard, I increasingly knew Fay would not be an insult to Sophie's intelligence. I intuited that Sophie would dig in her heels at any program that told her what to wear, what to listen to, what to think. She was bright, strong, and in crisis. She did not need to be rebuilt, only reoriented. This just might be possible with Fay. But the place itself? I couldn't get a clear sense of the setup. And Sophie would be one of the first to attend Northern Lights, along with a girl from California and one from Minnesota. I told myself I had to have a clear decision by the next day, as though the right decision, on hearing this, would pull itself together and manifest at that appointed time. I wished I could go and see the two programs, meet the people, make a more educated decision, but there wasn't time. There simply wasn't time. I had to decide sight unseen.

I called Stephen and asked him if he would come directly to my office when he arrived on Friday. I wanted to call the final two choices with him there, have him talk to the people, to see what his take was on the two options. I desperately needed a second opinion. Other than the educational consultant, I had been working in a total vacuum. He spoke to the contact at Marks Creek and then to Fay. Generally, Stephen will circle a point, like a dog anticipating lying down, tediously restating the supporting evidence over and again. But in this case there was no hesitation. "It's Fay, it's Montana," he said as he hung up. "Your instincts are right." Shaking, I picked up the phone and called Fay and told her we would be coming that weekend. I then called Trek West and asked if they would prepare Sophie for the fact that she wouldn't be returning home.

SIX

Headed for the High Line

The designated meeting place for the Trek West out-take was along the McKenzie River, a magnificent Oregon river. It careens recklessly off the steep western slope of the Cascades, plummeting down cliff faces, spewing curtains of mist and sounding the deep, unmistakable drum of water against submerged rock, until it settles into a comfortable lope on its way to the Willamette Valley. We gathered at a point where the river started to settle down, churning out final declarations of independence in sassy displays of white water. A campfire under the shelter of a canopy of ponderosa and tamarack was being coaxed to life by the returning trekkers. The parents were asked to remain in the parking lot until called over to the fire circle. We milled about as nervously as freshly penned cattle, pacing in between the parked cars, walking upriver a ways and turning abruptly on our heels back again. Several parents acknowledged one another in an effort to defuse the tension—greetings flimsy and inadequate and yet all we could manage. "How's it going?" "Any trouble on the drive over?" "How was the flight?" I couldn't play the small-talk game, so desperate was I to see Sophie and equally anxious about the tight schedule we had created to get to Montana as fast as possible before Sophie came to and realized she wasn't going home. We would go to Stephen's near Portland, let Sophie shower and change, fly out at 6:00 P.M., land in Great Falls at 10:00 P.M., rent a car and drive north, in the direction of the ranch, until we were too tired to go on. That would give Stephen and me the next morning to deposit Sophie and return to the Great Falls airport. I wanted to get her to Montana while she was still experiencing the euphoria of our being reunited, of feeling good about having what it took to tough it out in the cold, snowy mountains, of being drug free for three weeks, of confessing her worst moments to the group, and, thereby, freeing herself from the tyranny of those actions and decisions. And I had to keep her out of her father's reach. He had called with threats "to spring her." I needed to get her to Montana while I was still strong enough to carry out my decision. It felt as though I was being led along by an aspect of myself I hardly knew. I had to put my faith in that stranger, a woman of clarity, decisiveness, a woman of action, a woman who didn't second-guess herself or her best instincts.

I strained to pick Sophie out from among the ragged band clad in bulky parkas, hats, and mittens, longing to see her, to run to her, to hold her, to hold her. "What is taking so long?" I demanded of Stephen impatiently. Finally, we were signaled to come over. Someone might as well have yelled "Go!" We sprinted in heeled and hiking boots, street shoes and sneakers as one, toward the group huddled by the fire, calling out the names of our children. "Sophie!" There she was!

"Mam!" She smiled broadly out from under a woolen hat and galumphed toward me in her unwieldy boots and layers of winter clothing. We were completely overwhelmed by our happiness to see each other. Our hug was so densely packed with emotion it became unwieldy and awkward. There was so much to say we were tongue-tied, our feelings so charged we could barely touch on them. It was at once an I-love-you embrace, an I-missed-you-desperately, a thank-God-you're-safe embrace, the hug that follows after a nightmare, the consoling parent seated on the side of the bed, cradling the frightened child. We gathered all of this and more inside the circle of our arms. Wiping the tears from her eyes with the back of her sleeve, Sophie returned to her designated place in the circle around the fire directly across from Stephen and me. That gesture, and then how she folded her legs under her to sit, how she pulled her cuffs forward over her hands, waved a tiny, secret wave at me, cupped her chin—it was Sophie.

The counselor established that each child would take turns making a full disclosure of previous drug use, next offering an apology to parents, and finally, announcing a plan for his or her future. His presentation was interrupted by clumps of soggy snow dislodged by the heat of the fire from the evergreen canopy above, startling one or the other of us by landing on our heads or in the fire, setting up a smoky hiss. Smoke, if it follows beauty, found us all beautiful. Our eyes watered, our noses ran—as though they weren't anyway. The staff had pulled me aside to tell me Sophie had only learned the night before that she wouldn't be going home. They would have liked more time. "She cried most of the night," they reported, "but she seems better today."

I thought I had prepared myself for Sophie's disclosure. But I was shocked all over again by the extent of her use, the recklessness of her attitude, how intentionally destructive her actions were, like the McKenzie as it catapulted off the high reaches of the Cascades. Her penchant for risk taking and experimentation led her to try whatever was available. No cliff was too high—speed and acid providing risky complement to marijuana and alcohol. I was deeply moved by her apology to me, her longing to be understood, to regain my trust, to be my friend, to go home. I was heartbroken when she spoke of her father. She spoke softly, tenderly, articulating her understanding of his neediness, her wish for him to change, along with her realization she couldn't make that happen for him. It hurt so much to hear of what hurt her so much. It hurt to hear of what I hadn't been able to protect her from.

"And now for my plan." Referencing her trip-worn journal, clumsily turning the pages with her wool-gloved hand, she stopped to wipe her eyes and nose. "Actually," she shrugged, "actually, I guess it doesn't matter about my plan, because I'm . . . I'm not going home after all." She fought back tears. "I just was told yesterday so this plan doesn't fit where I am going. I'm not even sure where that is. . . . Montana somewhere . . ." Her voice drifted off. She explained she was proud of her plan, had been eager to try it out, wished that I would reconsider but knew I wouldn't. The counselor encouraged her to discuss what her personal goals were, that she had included in her plan—but even in her effort to single them out, separate them away from the whole, she kept returning to the picture she had carefully drawn of herself back at home, with me, doing well in school, not using, being involved in sports, returning to the piano, seeing a counselor. She cried as she struggled through what wouldn't be. I cried as I heard it, wishing I felt it were possible, knowing it wasn't, knowing I had to let go of her, send her away. A year, maybe less, that's all.

Out of deference to our tight schedule, Sophie had been allowed to present first. When she had finished, we silently left our places in the circle around the fire. We loaded up her things and headed toward Portland, soon colliding with the world of people and traffic. Sophie looked out at it as though from another planet. She sat in the back, I in the front. Stephen drove. I reached my hand back between the seats. She took it and held it. I felt my love for her course through my arm and out through my hand to her as palpably as an electrical current. We drove the three hours to Stephen's. I said little, so afraid something I might say would trigger her resistance to going to Montana. I didn't know if I had it in me to stand up to her. I didn't know if I had it in me to stand up to my own doubts about what I was doing.

She lingered in the hot shower yelling out cheerily how great it felt, how much she loved me, could she call Megan and Rachel, just where was this place in Montana, couldn't she please go home, how hungry she was. The tone of her voice was full bodied, full of Sophie, of life. She had returned to herself. I washed the clothes she wanted to keep from Trek West and laid out clean ones for her I had brought along. Once I saw the ranch in Montana, I had told myself, I would have a better idea of what she would need there, and so had packed only one suitcase with new, bright white underwear, socks, and some of her pants, shirts, and sweaters.

I imagined corrals reclaimed on the old place, as Fay described it. I imagined a small, tidy ranch house, not big enough to house the girls coming, and her widowed mother's off a ways, some extra available bedrooms now that her family was grown and gone. I pictured chickens, their feathers blowing inside out as they strutted before the wind. I could see an Australian shepherd with one blue eye, barking and wagging his tail; a machine shed with tractors tucked neatly inside for the winter. I pictured pickups burdened with hay bales for the next morning's feeding, sheets crisp-frozen on the clothesline. I pictured the Milk River that Fay said flowed nearby, lined with cottonwood and willow. I imagined the honk of pheasant flushed out of the underbrush, the whistle of chukar, the sullen sideways glance of the coyote as he trotted by, eyeing the sheep by the house, too close to the dogs for him to risk it. I pictured a fenced-in yard, the bright primary plastic colors of Fay's young son's toys, rude against the winter browns. Nothing fancy, like she said. We headed to the airport, got on the plane to Great Falls and sped through the enormity of the jet blackness, the earth beneath us sloughing indicators of human presence as we arced over Idaho into Montana.

Heading out of Great Falls in the rented car, there seemed to be even fewer signs of human presence than seen from the air. The highway ran dully ahead, arrow straight, the visual ticking of the center stripe hypnotic. The speed limit was only of concern passing through the small hamlets along the way. Sprig, Montana: population 50. Everything shut for and against the night. Our headlights briefly illuminated a sign on a tavern window advertising fresh eggs and worms and a call for "Hides For Vets" next to the neon invitation to drink Budweiser. I could get no sense of the landscape in the darkness other than the fact that there wasn't one. We didn't seem to climb or descend. No rise or fall in the broad chest of the land. My own breath was just as tightly held and would stay that way until I could know something about the place we were taking Sophie. She had thankfully fallen asleep in the car. I whispered to Stephen of my growing panic. It mounted in me like a backward birthing, moving up from the cradle of my pelvis, to my stomach and into my throat until I could only hug my ribs, rock in my seat, and groan.

Stephen was too exhausted to drive one more mile. We spotted a motel that was still open and pulled in next to a long row of semis, idling like snoring dragons to ward off the thickening effects of the subzero cold on their diesel fuel. We aroused Sophie and the three of us staggered into yet another bleak motel room on the night before handing my child off to strangers one more time. We muttered our goodnights and fell into bed. I silently cried myself to sleep.

The plastic lined curtains were drawn tightly shut, so I couldn't tell if it was morning. I went into the bathroom to find out and was terrified by what I saw out the window. Nothing. I could see as far as I could. Nothing, not a tree, not a hill, a bank, or knoll stood between me and the capacity of my vision. I was looking into Canada, maybe farther, across miles of wheat stubble. In the motel room, in the restaurant where we stopped for breakfast, in the town there seemed to be a campaign underway to prove that color didn't exist. Beige, relieved only by the gray tin of the grain silos that loomed roadside. Beige carpet, bedspreads. Beige buildings, cars, and clothes. I had ranched, nearly seventeen years, in both eastern Montana and Central Oregon's High Desert. Stark landscapes both. Could it be the strength of my fantasy about the ranching life had conjured intimate valleys where there were none, mirages of narrow, golden-walled canyons, rivers lined with pale-leafed cottonwoods? We got back into the car. I looked at Sophie in the back seat. She stared out the window. She said nothing. Neither did I.

We calculated we had thirty miles still to go to the turn into Fay's ranch. We crossed the Milk River on a single lane metal truss bridge. I was slightly calmed to see the ranches along the river looking more like what I had pictured as our destination. On one side of the highway, we had broken out of the grasp of the endless wheat fields. Instead, alfalfa, cows grazing, and in the distance, the Bear Paw Mountains rising, almost apologetically, from the sea of flatness. The mile markers ticked by. When I'd see a place that looked inviting— a red barn, tidy round corral, prim white house and hired man's cottage—I'd ask Stephen: "Is that it? Is that it?"

"Three miles to go," he said.

"Then that's it, right up there, that next one." I nudged Stephen.

We turned off the highway, paralleled on the other side by a railroad track, and on to a dirt road. The deep, frozen ruts tossed our rental car like a small skiff on a rough sea, the underside scraping against the high spots. We gunned it up a slight rise, the tops of tall cottonwood trees just coming into view. Cresting the hill, there was the ranch before us.

Piles of old machinery, snarls of discarded wire in heaps, a shed listing precariously, old tires stacked up against its wall, a small, jelly-bean shaped camper trailer with wooden blocks in front of its flat tires and the house—originally plastered on the outside, but by now enough of the plaster siding chipped off that the effect was mottled and unkempt. The yard had once been fenced—white, wooden stakes still standing with nothing to hold on to. Wooden pallets formed a makeshift boardwalk leading to the back door. A wolf-husky cross dog on a long chain had worn a deep circle in the dirt nervously tracing the limits of his freedom. He barked at the car as we drove in and sounded serious about it. Another mottled yellow dog, unchained, wagged over toward our car as we pulled up.

"Are you sure this is it?" I asked Stephen, unable to disguise my incredulity.

"Mile post 28. That's exactly where we turned," he replied.

"But there doesn't seem to be anyone here and she knows we're coming. I called her this morning." I wanted to bolt.

"It's going to be fine," reassured Stephen. "Go see if this is the right place."

I got out of the car and, braving the wolf dog, went to the door and knocked. I looked back at Stephen and Sophie who watched me, Sophie with her chin in her hand, her forehead leaning against the window. I knocked again. I could hear an interior door open and close. A young woman came to the door. I asked if this was the Northern Lights ranch.

"Yes it is."

"Are you Fay?"

"No. Hi, I am Jen." She extended her hand. "I work with Fay."

I realized it was the daughter of the man I had spoken to in Connecticut. The place was a work in progress he had said. "*No shit,*" I thought to myself. "Is Fay here?"

"Oh, yes. She's expecting you. She's on the phone just now. Come on in."

"I'll get the others," I said as confidently as I could. I stepped out the back door. The wolf dog shoved his nose in my crotch. I stumbled and stepped in the pie tin of dried dog food, scattering it across the dirt. Regaining my balance, I waved Stephen and Sophie in and called out: "This is it! Come on!" Stephen got out. Sophie stayed in the car. "Oh no," I muttered to myself, wondering if the keys were still in the car. I started toward her when a voice behind me said hello.

I turned and there in front of me was a full-figured woman of nearly six feet, or so she seemed, with long thick auburn hair that she had twisted on top of her head and skewered with a pencil. Her skin looked satin smooth despite its daily baptism by Montana weather and her eyes were the whisper green of winter sage. She had beautifully proportioned hands with long, capable fingers. She wore a sweatshirt and sweat pants of no particular color, thick glasses, and on her feet, slippers—large, brown, fuzzy slippers with antlers, an embroidered brown nose, and plastic eyes with small black beads for eyeballs that rolled around deliriously when she walked. "Hi," she said. "I'm Fay. Sorry to be on the phone. Come on in. Ellen? Stephen? Real pleased to meet you." She peered over my shoulder. "Sophie hanging in the car? Well, let's us go on in then."

I followed her dizzy moose feet across the back porch, most of which was taken up with a freezer, piles of galoshes, boot scrapers, empty plastic milk jugs, egg cartons, thirty-pound bags of dog food, milk replacer for calves, and buckets with various syringes for doctoring cattle poking out like porcupine quills. And on into the kitchen: A metal-legged table with a pale yellow Formica top claimed the center of the space, with ten chairs of assorted color, shape, and life expectancy arranged around it. Greasy kitchen magnets held notices of livestock auctions and yellowed grocery lists to the refrigerator. The telephone at the end of the counter, were it not hung on the wall, would have been crushed under the piles of catalogs; books on addiction, self-esteem, adolescence, codependence, and attachment disorder; and pamphlets on raising sheep and butchering hogs.

"Here. We can sit down in here." Fay gestured toward the living room. Boxes of her young son's toys and books lined the room. Neglected plants hung from the ceiling, suspended in dusty macramé plant hangars. A large print of an American Indian woman reclining on a Navajo blanket dominated one wall. "Do either of you need the bathroom before we get started? It's right there," she said, gesturing over her shoulder.

I accepted the offer and headed toward the door in the middle of the narrow hallway Fay had pointed to. Inside, the shelf above the toilet sagged beneath the weight of countless bottles of lotion, shampoo, Pepto-Bismol, Vaseline, hydrogen peroxide. Dirty laundry boiled over the top of the hamper. I rejoined Stephen and Fay in the living room feeling more and more anxious.

"So," began Fay, "how was the trip and how is Sophie doing?" For all the assuredness and confidence in her voice, we might as well have been sitting in a pristine corporate boardroom.

"OK, it seems, so far," I said nervously. "Shall I go get her?"

"I imagine she'll want to come in from the cold before too long." She paused a moment. "How much time do you have before you have to head out? I'd like to show you around."

"We have to leave in a couple of hours." Stephen stated.

"Well, we can talk for awhile here first and then we'll take a tour of the ranch and then drop Sophie off at my mother's where she'll be staying."

"Shall I go get Sophie?" I asked again, standing up robotically, not waiting for an answer. I got to the door to the back porch and met Sophie coming in. "Oh!" I said startled to see her. I half expected to see her driving away. That's what I wanted to do.

She walked in slowly, taking a lot of time to look around first the kitchen, then the hallway, and then gingerly stepping into the living room.

"Hey there, Sophie." Fay stood up and shook Sophie's hand. "I'm Fay. Welcome to Northern Lights."

Sophie sat down in the upholstered chair next to the sofa where Stephen and I were and directly across from Fay. We all were silent.

For a long time. Sophie scanned every detail of the room, the photographs on the table, the books on the shelves, the board games piled under the television stand, absent the television, and then, out the window at the prairie that took off down the driveway, across the highway, and on and on until the sky took up where the land left off.

"So, Sophie," Fay asked quietly, "do you think you could feel safe here?"

Sophie continued to stare out the window, remaining so still I wasn't sure she had heard the question. She then turned her head slowly, bringing her attention back into the room, and looked squarely at Fay. It was as though she realized the answer she chose, and her responsibility to it, must be handled with extreme care. "Yes. I think so," she finally answered. "Yes. I think I could."

SEVEN

Leaving Sophie at the Bar

The tour began with a drive farther down the highway and into a neighboring ranch. Fay jolted her pickup to a halt on the top of a hill. "There it is," Fay said proudly. Stephen, Sophie, and I looked. Jacked up on blocks was an enormous pale green three-story house with white trim. On one side a porch had been sheared off, leaving a scar of exposed wood. A door hung cock-eyed from a single hinge. All the windows were broken. "It will be moved next week, set on that hole you saw dug out there at my place. I got it for the cost of moving it." She enthusiastically talked about her plans for renovating the house, how it would comfortably accommodate the total number of girls she anticipated having at Northern Lights, as well as her family and an office. The house, she explained, gesturing at the shabby structure before us, had a spacious dining room, living room, and kitchen as well as a basement that she would convert into a den and, where the porch had been, she would build a solar-heated interior green house. That she could, in her imagination, convert the up-rooted relic teetering on railroad ties into such a place of promise seemed incredulous and unrealistic to me. Sophie stared out the window, her chin in her hand, and said nothing.

"When do you think it will be done?" I asked, Fay's optimistic description reminding me of the books of my childhood in which, the very next morning, the heroine awoke to find the formerly neglected house all sparkling new, white curtains in the window and fresh baked pies cooling on the sill.

"I'm hoping within the year."

Sophie will never see it finished, I thought to myself.

"Biggest obstacle is getting workmen out here. There's only one dang plumber for the whole county, one sheet rock guy, one electrician, one carpenter. Girls and I, we'll be able to do some of it."

We drove back along the highway slowly, with Fay pointing out their dry land wheat, rye, and irrigated alfalfa; the pasture that had good wind breaks and protection reserved for lambing and calving, and, off in the distance, where they turned out the pairs during the summer. We pulled off the highway again, this time over the railroad tracks on the opposite side from Fay's and headed toward Canada. I came to think of it that way, as there was nothing of significance between where we were and the border seventy miles north, other than steel cattle guards every section or so. We turned and drove into a compound that included a doublewide trailer, a white farmhouse, a loafing shed, and a barn with ramshackle corrals attached. "The white house," Fay explained, "is where Jen stays—you met her back at the house. No one is in the doublewide right now. The loafing shed is where the pigs are and the back section there is where we'll put any bummer lambs. Sooner than you think and we'll be in the thick of lambing and calving."

At this point I was desperate to find something I could attach to that looked complete, done with care and attention to detail, orderly. I wanted an indicator, anything, of what Fay's idea of finished was. How could she help resolve my daughter's chaos if she lived in chaos herself? Everything seemed to be a work in progress. The closest I could come was the doublewide. I seized on it. "Why don't you all live in the trailer? It looks *clean* and *nice*," I emphasized clean and nice, "with a lovely view, ready to go." I said this in a tone that implied Fay hadn't considered what to me was the obvious. Fay wasn't fazed by my insinuation. "It's hard to heat, and the water's not hooked up. Needs a lot of work. Just don't know yet." I couldn't see anything that didn't need a lot of work. Sophie remained troublingly silent. I projected she had resigned herself to being left in this godforsaken place. I wanted her to react, show some sign of life. I guessed she thought I had lost my mind, that it wasn't worth protesting, things had gotten so weird. I imagined she must be in shock, having just come off three weeks of a hard scrabble wilderness experience only to find herself here. My dread at leaving her made me more and more frantic to get things just so before going, to shape this experience, to take control of the situation so I could know the outcome. But nothing was cooperating. Nothing was falling into place.

"We'll go back to the house so you can get your car and then we'll go on to Mom's," Fay announced. "We'll meet the rest there."

My stomach jumped. It would soon be time to leave Sophie. I wasn't sure I could. I only just was reunited with her. And this felt so foreign, so messy, so unknown, so nothing, so absolutely without any reassuring signs of promise, so not a program, so not measurable steps. It was wrong. How could I know, could Fay know, could Sophie know if progress was being made? And who were "the rest," I asked. Fay explained we'd meet Rayleen, the teacher for Northern Lights, and the program's counselor, Hazel, who moved there from New York State. "Also Lana, who arrived two weeks ago from California. Debby, coming in from Minnesota, won't arrive for another week. That will give me time to help Sophie get situated."

We went back to the house. Stephen, Sophie, and I got into the rental car and followed Fay back out on to the highway. I looked in the side mirror and saw the mottled yellow dog give up the chase, tail wagging. Sophie had said almost nothing the whole time.

"What do you think?" I asked her.

"Whatever," her terse reply.

"Think this will be OK?" Like she could know.

"Whatever."

Fay had pulled off the two-lane road alongside an old building with two large front windows with a door in the center and a false front above the door that extended six feet or so above the flat roof. Wide concrete steps led up to the front door. A painted sign over the door said Hitching Post Bar.

"Why in the world are we stopping here?" I asked, feeling shell-shocked. We followed Fay, who had walked around behind the building. "*Why* are we here?" I asked Stephen and Sophie, or anyone and everyone.

Fay gestured to us from the back doorstep of the building. I went in first. Fay stood inside with her hands on the small, narrow shoulders of a little boy wearing a western cowboy shirt with mother of pearl snaps that were snapped out of order. "This is my son, Rory."

"Hi," Rory said brightly. "Are you Sophie? Are you the new girl? I have a new shirt, see?"

Sophie acknowledged Rory with a smile.

"I'd like you to meet my mom," Fay said. Entering the room from the front of the building, where I presumed the bar was, came Phyllis. To me she had the traditional look of a rural Montana woman—polyester pants, a floral overblouse disguising the slight loss of figure, a string of beads around her neck with matching earrings, neatly styled hair. She looked to be someone who had baked a lot of apple cobblers, wasn't easily rattled, had not traveled too far from where she was that very moment, and didn't care. She said hello to each of us, stood with the group for awhile, and then went back to her work.

Fay went down the hall and stood at the top of the stairs that led into the basement and called: "Lana! Come on up!" A delicate and pretty girl with her dark brown hair cropped in a short pixie cut emerged shyly from down below. She said hello, sat down on the sofa in the room we were in, and then, as though she'd forgotten something, slithered back downstairs. Fay said, "We can follow her to see where Sophie will be staying. They'll be down there together. Ron and I are upstairs with Rory across from my mom's room and the bathroom."

In the roomy basement three mattresses were lined up against one wall. Lana had already made a nest for herself. A down-filled comforter inside a flannel, plaid duvet covered her bed. A small pillow with a white satin slip and a handful of stuffed animals were arranged at the head. She shrugged a greeting to Sophie. Sophie smiled uncertainly at her.

I looked around, and all I could conclude was that everything I had planned on, dreamed of, was more and more fractured at every turn on this absurd tour of homes. Every sagging gate, abandoned doublewide, weathered out-building, makeshift bedroom, ring-stained bath tub—and now a decrepit bar! Everywhere I saw impossibility. Every unrealized dream for my child done my way, according to my principles, standards, and values, became further and further out of the question. What *was* the question? I didn't remember. I know: I'd quit my job, devote myself to Sophie and her recovery—we'd do it together. I could do it. I'd make it work somehow. I didn't need someone else, some program, something outside of myself. Didn't I trust my own instincts? Didn't I believe I was good enough, capable, smart, mother enough? Didn't I believe the universe would line up behind me and make ends meet if I turned myself over to Sophie? No. I didn't.

I followed Fay upstairs, leaving Sophie with Lana in the basement, and unleashed all my anxiety on her. "*This* is where Sophie will stay? It's a *bar*! How can you have girls stay in a bar, girls who are trying to get over substance abuse?" I hissed.

"I'm working on their abuse, and why they made the choices they did, not the fact that substance exists in the world," Fay replied calmly. "And it's true, this is a bar, *and* this is a Montana bar. That means it is a place where people come for eggs, milk, food, mail, UPS deliveries, and just to gather. The kids roller skate on the big open floor. We have dances here. And, yes, locals will stop for a beer or two."

I was raging inside. *How could this woman claim she had a program, was ready to take on girls! Nothing is ready. The whole thing is makeshift. How could this possibly be a better solution than having Sophie at home?* I wanted . . . what did I want? I wanted this to be easy, to turn out right, just this once.

Fay announced: "Looks like Rayleen and Hazel are here. Rayleen will be coordinating the schooling for the girls—all their credits—whether they home school or go to the local high school. She has her master's and is a certified teacher. Hazel is the counselor and will also help teach some of the home-school classes as well as organize some special projects and field trips."

I reluctantly followed Fay into the front of the building, dragging a growing load of attitude behind me. It was a huge room, with ceilings at least eighteen feet high, dwarfing anyone in it. Most everything in and about Montana so far seemed to have that effect. The light from the two large front windows didn't make it halfway to the back wall. On one side of the room was an elaborate wooden bar. Six stools with swiveling red linoleum seats patched with duct tape were unoccupied. Behind the bar was an enormous, ornately framed mirror. Above it was an array of posters, some with shapely and half clad women drinking something or other, others with homilies like: "Don't squat with your spurs on!" showing a cartoon cowboy, pants around his ankles, reacting to the uncomfortable discovery that he had. Other than the bar and a few tables, a large wooden dance floor claimed one half of the room, a pool table the other. Phyllis sat at one of the tables by the window with two other women whom Fay introduced to me and Stephen as Hazel and Rayleen. They stopped their conversation and looked up at me. I felt I had interrupted them and was irritated I felt that way. My God! I had traveled 1,000 miles, was delivering my child to their care under very traumatic circumstances, and this was the reception I got? Fay again described, only this time in their presence, what their functions would be. I watched them to make sure they didn't react as though this was the first time they'd heard anything of it. I looked at Rayleen and wondered if the future of my daughter's education was in capable hands with her. I was only dimly aware of all the prejudiced assumptions I was working under—that no school in a place like this could be any good, nor any of the teachers in it. That no one worth their salt would move here from New York to be a counselor. I had little to say to them. I had drawn my own conclusions.

I gestured frantically to Stephen to follow me outside. We stepped out into a freezing wind. "This is crazy! Stephen, look at this! Look at this. A bar! How can I leave Sophie here? Fay lied. She didn't tell me about this. And those other women! Who are *they*?"

Stephen didn't interrupt my tirade; instead, like lunging a colt, he let me prattle until I ran to the end of my own rope. "Give it a try," he said. "If it doesn't work, you can always come get her. Give it a try."

"Oh my God," I bawled. The wind blew across my open mouth like someone blowing across an empty bottle, making a little whistle sound.

"Here." Stephen gestured toward the car. "Let's get Sophie's things inside. We have to leave in a few minutes." He put his hand gingerly on my shoulder, like someone handling a live grenade.

I carried in one suitcase with Stephen carrying another behind me. We deposited them near one of the beds in the basement. Sophie refused my offer to make her bed. I went back upstairs and lamely asked Fay to let me know what Sophie would need in the way of clothing or things for her room. Things for her room. What a joke. Things for her room. A stereo, posters of handsome young male actors, clever quotes, a bulletin board of photos, of friends at camp, on the ski slope, an alarm clock, a stack of school books, an assignment book. Wrong dorm, wrong school. Sophie was enrolled in a very different curriculum. Life school. I started crying. Fay put her hand on my arm. "Sophie's needs will be met here, Ellen. *Sophie's* needs," she repeated gently but firmly in a liquid alto voice that had soothed heifers while she extracted their first calf from between their narrow hips, quieted high-strung colts. "And among those is a port in the storm, a place to heal. That's what this is. I know it's hard for you to see that just now."

Rory, who stood next to his mother, looked up and asked me: "Is Sophie staying here with us? And do you want her to? Why are you crying? Why is this sad?" I couldn't answer him.

I went down into the basement to say good-bye to Sophie. To my surprise, she had already made her bed. Humphrey lay splayed across her pillow, his worn brown head lolling off to one side, his smile outlined in black yarn offering the same steady encouragement it always did. She was talking to Lana. Maybe she didn't realize what was happening. Why wasn't she protesting? Didn't she hate this? She followed me outside. I was sobbing. I felt so afraid of what I didn't, couldn't know. We held each other. Sophie started to cry. I thought then it was because she was sad. I now think she did because she finally could, as much and for as long as she needed, without concern for me or her father, without the worry that if she allowed herself to fall to pieces there would be no one to pick them up. I now think she had already decided Fay would be there for her and it was safe to cry. "Bye, Mam." I didn't say: "If you don't like it you can come home." I didn't say that. Should I have? I didn't say: "You'll be fine, everything's going to be fine." I didn't say "I'll see you soon" or "We'll talk soon" or "Hang in there." What I said was, "I love you."

EIGHT

Distance Learning

Stephen must have felt he was in the company of a lunatic on the drive back to Great Falls. I would alternately sob and rail about what I had just done—oblivious to any response he might offer. Then I'd abruptly stop midsentence and retreat into catatonic silence, gazing at a horizon that remained static despite our terrible speed. Giant wooden windbreaks that protected the highway from blowing snow materialized along the road like the unearthed spine of some prehistoric beast, providing my imagination brief reprieve from my own squalling grief. My soggy pile of Kleenexes grew, eventually spilling out from the inside of the door pocket. There's something about blowing one's nose that takes the edge off grief. It is such a practical and remedial action and implies a willingness, in the midst of disaster, to do something on one's behalf. There was hope for me.

What Stephen had been patiently repeating like a mantra, as regularly as the mile posts flew by, was that this was better than bringing Sophie back home and, who knew, maybe *much* better. "What does he know?" I thought to myself bitterly. "He doesn't even have kids." My ability to listen to reason was bullied by fear. I wanted to blame him, someone. I wanted just one other person to be exactly me, thereby validating my misery, to know and understand what I was feeling and what's more—to explain it to me, so we'd both know. But like Sophie on her way to Trek West, there soon was a lack of conviction in my tears. Like a warm chinook wind that coaxes

threads of water from underneath the frozen snow, slowly an awareness of what I had done settled over me. I began to relax. We had
gotten her there. She was safe. At the very least, her basic needs
would be met.

And what of this odd place and assortment of people who
would be designing my daughter's days? They in combination would
not let me organize their parts into any sort of whole, would not
permit me the false sense of being in charge or control. *What I could
do,* I thought to myself, *is turn around and go back and get Sophie. Or,* I
countered, *what I could do was try trusting on for size, trusting my decision, trusting Fay.* I chose what had become the least familiar path—
trust.

After turning in the rental car and flying together from Great
Falls, Stephen said good-bye to me at the Portland airport, and I
took the shuttle on to Bend. The silence in my empty house engendered low-grade panic. Where was my companion chaos?
Where was the steady diet of high-decibel emotions, my idea of
the music of family, my idea of normal. Craziness had become so
familiar, I felt more crazy without its presence. Though this trip
had been short in actual time, it felt eons in metaphorical time. I
wandered through the house, lingering briefly in each room just
to reorient myself. First, Sophie's empty bedroom, which had begun to take on the odor of an uninhabited space and the look of
one: the bed perfectly made, the knick-knacks I had obsessively
arranged in meticulous formation on top of her bookshelf while
she was at Trek West, her bureau top clear of any evidence of an
occupant. I had organized the things in her room into describing
my idea of a successful young woman on her way. It would turn
out to be true, only it wouldn't be my idea.

I walked past the door to the children's bathroom, past Isabelle's
and Nick's rooms, which also stood abandoned—Isabelle back at
college and Nick having returned to his job in Squaw Valley. Mine
was the room at the foot of the stairs, chosen so I could monitor
their adolescent comings and goings. They had made a mockery of
that plan, I learned, sliding off the roof to slip away in the night to

parties. I continued my tour in the living room. The photographs were still in the same place on the coffee table, still broadcasting the same framed moments in time, still orienting my gaze, my position in the room, according to their angle. The furniture had not budged. To what extent did the objects in my house define me? I position them here and there, but don't they then, in concert with one another, start to dictate my movement through space, direct my memories in one direction or another? When do household objects become the co-conspirators in a fixed outlook? The kitchen, too, had waited in state for me to return. The only things that hadn't were the cucumbers and the milk in the fridge, now sour.

I reestablished contact with my mercurial cats—easily done with the aid of foul-smelling cat food—and glanced at the tree planted by the kitchen window to confirm that the frayed blue dog collar was still hanging from the branch, a memorial to our dog of sixteen years. Not only had the human population of this house decreased dramatically, but so had other life forms. We at one point had reached a high of a student living in the basement room, my three children, myself, various boyfriends (one at a time, please), and a mother's helper. Add to that two dogs, three guinea pigs, a parakeet, two cats, two goldfish, a chicken (which the children found in the neighboring park—how good of the city park to offer such a rural welcome), and Sophie's 4-H pig, which we transported in a gunny sack in the back of my station wagon to weigh-ins and meetings. And now this, an all-time low—two cats and me. No more students in the basement, the kids all scattered, Stephen on weekends only, no more mother's helpers, the remaining guinea pig given away after the other two ate each other during Nick's grade-school show-and-tell. The parakeet, who spent his life trying to get out of his cage, finally succeeded in lifting up his cage door with his beak, only to be eaten by the cat. The goldfish died—too much fluctuation in water temperature. The chicken was delivered to a friend's farm. The pig was Christmas dinner on the winning 4-H bidder's table. Eiffel, our dog who was especially devoted to Sophie, was the one we put down at age sixteen. And my beloved shepherd dog, Jet, I had temporarily returned to the ranch early on in the divorce, so disoriented was she by living in town. Once we were more settled, I went back to get her. Her carcass lay next to the corral. My former husband had shot her.

Telephone conversations with Sophie at Northern Lights were enviably filled with the background noise of a full household—one animal or another congenially mewing or barking; Lana, Debby, Fay, Rory, and Ron chattering; the clattering of dishes or the slam of the storm door. Initially communicating with Sophie by any means was awkward and unwieldy. Without seeing her, I couldn't read the intonations in her voice, pick up hidden messages. She was, I was certain, miserable or sad or contemplating escape. It couldn't be that she was OK and simply reporting the activities of the day. Fay reminded me repeatedly that it was important to take what Sophie said at face value, not to impose more meaning, my meaning, on it. "If you do that, you don't hold her as able to express her own feelings. If you do that, you give her an excuse not to be clear with herself. Then, if she feels misunderstood, she'll have you, once again, to blame." It was painful to acknowledge my role in what Sophie was working through. Sophie's issues were not the result of spontaneous combustion. If, as parents, we are going to insist our kids ask themselves the tough questions, then we are going to have to look inside ourselves with the same rigor and honesty we are demanding from our children.

The ranch had only one phone. Fay explained she could better monitor the calls that way. But between Fay's telephone conferences with other parents, ranch business, and the girls calling their families, the phone was often busy. After trying six times or so over the course of a day I would give up in frustration. I missed Sophie madly. I was worried about her and made myself miserable second-guessing what I had done. I needed to hear from Fay how Sophie was doing, and even more, to hear from Fay how I was doing. In my withdrawal from chaos and dysfunction, my hand would reach for the phone prompted by every, any emotional configuration—fear, frustration, doubt, paranoia, loneliness, anger. My children were all far gone and the man I was in a relationship with lived and worked in a city three hours from me, as if I had driven them all away. I saw this as something wrong that I needed to change, instead of accepting it as the universe organizing itself in such a way that I could have time to reflect and heal. Had things come together like this on my behalf? Maybe this was that elusive idea my brother had expressed when he talked about letting life bounce me back. Instead, I persisted in adding everyone's distance to my evidence list of being unworthy, unwanted, and left behind. But could it be possible that out of a subconscious honoring of my process, they had made room for me? And (could I handle this?) that Sophie needed distance from me for her healing as much as I needed space in order to do the same?

In my frustration at not being able to speak with Fay when I wanted to, and my superior conclusion that I knew how to organize things and she didn't, I tried to force a system on her, tried to get her to call me at the same time each week or send a weekly written evaluation instead of the monthly one she proposed. But inevitably one of the girls needed some special attention or a family meeting (when they all sat down together to discuss a particular issue) ran longer than expected. What she was telling me was that I was one of a number of priorities, and not a high-ranking one. Sophie and the other girls in her care took precedence over all else. The withdrawal I experienced was in proportion to my attachment to my daughter as a substitute for living my own life—having no voice in her day-to-day life felt like radical surgery. I wanted it to be me, in an active sense, that made at least *some* of the difference. I wanted the credit. In pressing Fay for a set telephone time, in insinuating that the trailer house might be nicer, cleaner, in lunging at ways, no matter how inconsequential, of measuring Sophie's progress, I was under the illusion that through externally imposed systems I could still control Sophie's environment and, thereby, Sophie: her process, the conclusions she would reach, and the life she would lead. I was so dead wrong.

Each time I hung up the phone, and the silence of my house overwhelmed me again and again, I saw that the present company was the focus, none other. My task was to hold my children and myself as able, to actively participate in my own love and pursuit of life and watch, bemusedly, as the lives of those I had helped bring into the world unfolded. Though I credited myself for standing by, never wavering, my absence was as critical to Sophie's healing as was her father's. It was so hard for me to speak this as it suggested that her father and I were partners (not equal, but partners nevertheless) in the problems our children were having. It was central to my belief system that he, his disease, was the evil element and I, the Joan of Arc, was warring for the good. Maybe so, but a war-torn environment, no matter what the reason, is not the setting needed to heal. Sophie needed to find Sophie. And I needed to find myself.

Woven increasingly into our conversations were Sophie's references to Fay. "Fay says . . ." "I don't think Fay would like it." "I'll ask Fay." I was unprepared for my territorial and jealous reaction to Fay replacing me in the mother role. And Sophie seemed so willing to place her trust in Fay in a way I didn't feel I had ever experienced. I felt gypped big time. Fay gently explained that she was baggage-free in Sophie's eyes. She held no expectations but simply was there to witness and guide, which freed Sophie, created the emotional environment necessary for Sophie to start unburdening herself. Sophie, Fay explained, was, like me, suddenly without the scapegoats she relied on—me, her peers, her father. "I'm here to watch, to guide Sophie's growing realization of having only herself to turn to, to reclaim, and eventually to celebrate." I felt pathetically alone when Fay said this, wondering what caring and wise person was watching over me as I struggled to reconstruct.

My first significant act of self-reclamation was to move my office into the house. It would save me money—as I was faced with the large monthly tuition to Fay—and allow me to work late if needed. But most importantly it would facilitate my own writing, which I had returned to as if returning to a long-lost lover. I created an altar to the muse on the shelf above my computer, carefully placing various talismans: a music box from a friend, a dried autumn leaf stamped with "Made entirely with recycled materials" from a fellow writer, a small Alaskan bear carved of soapstone and inlaid with turquoise Stephen had given me, a scented candle. This motley collection was the first outward expression, barely a whisper, of an interior change in my view of the world and my place in it.

When the children were small if I had to be away from them for any length of time, I'd describe the length of my absence in terms of Sesame Streets. "I'll be back in one Sesame Street," I'd assure them, and I'd head out to move cattle, help in the corrals, weigh in pungent loads of potato silage on the truck scales. Having given instructions to the babysitter, I'd leave them curled up in front of the hazy transmission of Kermit and Oscar on the only station the gnarled antenna on our roof was able to snag on its wiry tentacles.

A few weeks into Sophie's stay at Northern Lights, I got a letter from her:

> Our last conversation wasn't the best. I know I should be able to admit when you're right but sometimes I wish you weren't, and other times you're not. The reason I'm so irritated, not irritated, pissed that I'm here is because when I was at Trek West I thought I was going to be able to come home. I was inspired with the things I was going to do . . .
>
> I just wish I could have an idea of when I can come home. . . . I just wish someone would tell me how many Sesame Streets I have to be gone.

On the eve of putting the finishing touches on my altar, the phone rang. It was Sophie.

"Hey." Her voice was lifeless, flat.

"Sophie, hi!"

"This place is a dump and I hate it. I *hate* it! Why did you make me come? I want to come home. The house has been moved, and we're crammed in the basement, and it's a mess. Every box elder bug in the world has been hibernating in these walls and they are all crawling stupidly around. They're everywhere—my clothes, my shoes, my toothbrush. It's gross. It's totally gross!"

I instantly drained my small reserve of confidence trying to give encouragement, help her to see the need to do the hard work. I had only just begun myself. It would take us both more Sesame Streets than either of us could count. I suggested she could organize, decorate, and keep *her* room clean the way she wanted, her own special space, her own altar. The rest, I speculated with her, she couldn't control, unless she wanted a full-time job as a housekeeper, something I could tell her a thing or two about. She wasn't ready to hear any of it—much less from a slightly enlightened mother, a mother with a trace of self in her voice, not to mention humor. It was still important to her to place all I said in a box labeled "Whatever" or "Gimme a Break" or "Get off My Back" or "All Not Seeing, All Not Knowing." I was placed on the planet to react to, not to heed.

But in a call a few weeks later, her tune had changed. "Mom, you won't believe it! So cool. We built a sled and hooked it up to the snowmobile. Fay pulled me and Debby and Lana around—and Rory. You should have seen Lana. I don't think she'd ever, like, been in snow before. I've never laughed so hard. So fun! Phyllis made us venison stew. Oh, and the coolest thing! Hazel told me about putting fresh herbs in a tea ball and floating the tea ball in the bath tub to make my own herbal bath. I tried it. I'm just hangin' with Fay tonight. It's butt cold, like thirty below at night. I mean, try feeding cattle in this temperature!"

Sophie's life in Bend had reduced itself to associating exclusively with her peers, with little to no contact with any other age group or philosophical perspective. Many of us fall prey to this, even within our families, separating out functions, child from child, child from adult. Kids off to programs, parents to work. Hire the parenting out. When I got my cell phone, it felt like remote parenting: "This is 617-5410 approaching driveway on Albany Street, do you read? Please be on doorstep with all you need for the rest of your life because I am about to drop you off somewhere." The ghettoization according to wealth and age. The monocultures artificially created by premeditated neighborhoods. Sophie was now experiencing the richness of a community of people, of interaction, of ages and activities. She was also being given the opportunity to remember what her own hands, in combination with her imagination, could do. What, with peace and quiet and time to ponder, she could invent.

I confessed to Fay on the phone the next day: "Damn it, Fay. I want to come and see Sophie—for all the right reasons and some wrong ones."

"Can you wait for her to ask you? Try not to fill in the blank before she even realizes it's a blank."

"Do you have any idea how hard this is, Fay?" I moaned.

"I have some," her reply.

I waited. And waited some more. It was early March. "Mam! Hi! Wait, hold on." I could hear a muffled commotion through the receiver. "Can you hear this?" I listened. At first I heard nothing, then . . . a small snorkeling grunt. "Did you hear that? The sow won't take two of her piglets, so we've got them in a box in the kitchen, and we're taking care of them. They are *so* cute. When I let them out they follow me everywhere! It's like I'm their mother." She paused. "I miss you, Mam. I want you to come and see me. When can you come?"

NINE

Painting with Light

In working out the details of the visit, Sophie and I talked more often, breaking down the barrier of the telephone somewhat, and once or twice even achieving an ease of exchange I hadn't had with her in over a year. Sour watermelon candies and olive bread ranked high on her list of requests of what to bring. She was using her camera a lot, she said. Did I still have any of the old dark room supplies? I told her I could round up materials for a primitive darkroom setup, so she could develop film and make contact sheets, but nothing fancier than that.

When the children were younger, I volunteered as a 4-H leader in photography for some of the neighboring ranch kids. I had worked as a photographer before I was married so it was familiar territory. Our "4-H Snapshooters" display of homemade cameras, and the images taken with them, won at the county fair. I had the children make pinhole cameras out of various shaped boxes. They painted the insides with flat, black paint. They then cut a small square out of one end and covered it with a piece of tin foil taped down on all sides. Next they surgically pierced the center of the tin foil with a straight pin and finally, folding a piece of tape back on itself, made a "lens cover" to keep the light out of the inside of the box until they were ready. We fashioned a dark room in the closet of the feedlot scale house where I daily dispatched feed and cattle trucks. All eight in the club, ranging in age from four (Sophie) to twelve (including Isabelle and Nick), squeezed inside the small room. They were giddy with the intrigue and mystery of being backstage in a darkened theater just before the curtain was to go up on a performance they were prepared for but couldn't know the outcome of. We placed rolled bath towels secured with black tape around the door frame, turned off the yellow safe light, and loaded each box with a single sheet of light-sensitive paper. The children, now adapted to the darkness, then taped the lids of their boxes down, so no light could leak in. Once everyone was ready, we opened the door, our eyes blinded by the sudden rush of daylight, and ran outside. It was almost impossible to accurately aim the cameras. But they thought they could, and would prop their box on the side of a rock or on a discarded tire and then lie down on the ground behind it to get a better sense of what they were aiming at, like a golfer lining up a difficult putt. They counted one-one thousand, two-one thousand up to ten as we had rehearsed, and then they covered the pinhole with the piece of tape and scrambled back to the dark room. In their imaginations they pictured their final product—the entire alfalfa field that lay below the feed pens, a magpie flying by, the lone heifer in the pen. In the darkroom, as the images slowly emerged in the tray of developer, it took them a while to figure out what they had, in fact, photographed. It was a negative image, first of all, so what was light was dark, and dark light. Maybe the sharp edge of the corral with the head of the heifer only just visible; maybe the phone pole, instead of the magpie flying by; maybe the harrow in the foreground, instead of the alfalfa field. Though the image wasn't what they had thought it would be, they weren't disappointed. The impact of light on the light-sensitive material was like magic to them. And then the funny thing of the image being a negative one, for them inside out, and upside down. I talked to them about light and dark, how light affected the surface of the paper. But in their young faces—as we looked at the results of our day's labor at the end of class, wet sheets of printing paper hung like a string of fish from clothespins on a line suspended across the room—I could see a kind of beyondness, an otherness as they contemplated what it meant for each of them that what they thought they saw wasn't all there was to see. That light, or maybe even other things, could play across their reality in such a way that it showed up differently than they could recognize or know.

Sophie was a "Snapshooter" graduate, asking now for the tools to return to exploring the reversal of image, how light and darkness can play tricks, that what we see is not always what we get. And other questions—like what of our own available light do we and don't we cast, and what of our experience is permanently etched on our light-sensitive souls? And outcome, what about that, the not know-ing and just remaining curious and respectful of all the ways light can play on reality? As for me, I only just began to grasp the implica-tions of what I had professed to teach. As for Sophie, she was hungry to remember what she once knew.

This time the drive to Northern Lights was remarkable only to the extent that it was so unlike the first trip. It was like retracing what I recalled as a trauma but in which I could now find elements of safety and even good news. A little drowsy, I pulled into the café at Sprig to get a cup of coffee. The owner sat behind the counter on a stool watching the TV suspended from the ceiling. Various hand-crafted items were arranged inside the glass case: dolls with enor-mous handknit skirts and pink, grotesque plastic faces, crocheted afghans, a vest made out of beer can parts. I handed him a dollar bill. He never stated the cost of the coffee, instead made the change and then inquired: "Is it goin'?" I fell awkwardly into the stride of his question. "It's goin'," I assured him and left. Maybe that's really all there is to it, I mused.

Sooner than I thought possible I saw the telltale profile of the Bow grain silo against the horizon. I felt almost sick with anticipa-tion as I approached the ranch turn. I still longed for the picture per-fect ranch, and it still wasn't. Although *some* progress had been made, for there it was—the enormous green house. It had been moved, al-though portions of the siding had been damaged in transit, the front porch broken off. The house sat exposed, like a tall, ungainly adoles-cent, still unincorporated into its surroundings. The frozen ground leading up to the house was mud, no opportunity for landscaping since the move was made. I had told Sophie and Fay I would prefer to sleep in the house, rather than in a motel in town—to save money and give me a better sense of what Sophie's living situation was like. My arrival set off a chorus of barks from Highway and Cochise, the dogs I had met some months ago. The slick rental car looked out of place next to the array of ranch vehicles, each bearing muddy testimony to how hard they worked.

I so badly did not want to start where Sophie and I had left off, did not want conjecture or projection to be the basis of my response to her. But with no opportunity to practice skills I only imagined having, I couldn't help myself. Sophie came jetting out the door. We hugged, and as we did, I could feel myself trying to scan what she was feeling, orienting myself based on guesses instead of standing my own emotional ground, or even knowing what it was. Against my body, Sophie felt tentative. Did she think I felt that way? She felt nervous. Was she? Sophie picked up my suitcase and invited me in for a tour. Fay was waiting at the door, ready to offer a hug by way of a hello. A hug from Fay is the consummate hug. The only thing she has on her mind at the moment of the hug is hugging. Sounds simple? Try it. I, with the best of intentions, just had.

The new girls lived in a dorm setting on the third floor. Sophie and Lana had the basement rooms, which were more private. Fay and her family were on the second floor. I was to sleep in an extra room there. The ground floor housed the kitchen, dining, and living rooms—all of which still begged for finishing work—sheet rock to put up, cabinets to finish installing. It was a chaotic, cheerful, unbelievable mess. The baby pigs were barely containable in their boxes, clamoring to get out, especially when they heard their adoptive mothers' voices. They would dodder after the girls, grunting pleasurably, their tiny hooves tick-tacking on the wooden floor, until they got stranded at the foot of the stairs, which caused frantic snorts and squeals at being left behind. Piles of homework and folded laundry waited hopefully for rightful owners. And, just as Sophie had reported, hoards of box elder bugs careened against the insides of the windows, aroused from a deep winter's sleep. The move seemed to have done nothing to inspire sorting through the stacks of books and papers on all possible emotional, veterinary, and mechanical disorders. It was as though each pile had been carefully transported just as it had been in the other house and placed on the new kitchen counters.

As I was introduced to each of the girls—four more had joined Sophie and Lana—I felt as though I should know how to play the visiting mother role in this situation, felt certain other mothers knew what to do. Take everyone out to dinner? Take Sophie somewhere special? Bring clever gifts for everyone? I did none of these. I simply wanted to see Sophie, hold her, and see, smell, touch the environment she was in. I simply wanted to be seen, held, and reminded that I could feel, could make contact with her. We flopped together on her bed while she showed me some snapshots of some of the things she had done since coming: in a canoe on the Missouri River; sitting in the window of the barn feeding an orphaned lamb a bottle of milk. Sophie was squarely in these photographs, looked directly at the camera. She clearly began to have pride in who she was, how she looked, to know she was pretty. She no longer felt the need to take scissors to her face. She held up one of her running alone, full stride, both feet airborne, like a ballerina, solo, leaping across the empty stage of the prairie. An Australian Shepherd followed her in a sideways, entertained, off-kilter way—one ear up, the other down, tail caught midwag. "I felt so good, Mam, so free doing that. It was right after I got here. You won't believe it, and don't tell anyone at home, but I'm starting to really love country and western. Here, listen to this." She put a CD on full volume. The Dixie Chicks. We listened to them sing about the need for "wide-open spaces to make the big mistakes." Sophie and I looked at each other, our eyes filling with tears. It was true for both of us, the wide-open spaces had been the backdrop for the big mistake-making and now the healing. Same big space. Same big sky.

We heard Fay calling to come and help get dinner on the table. We all mustered in the kitchen. Once seated before heaps of mashed potatoes, lamb chops, and homemade rolls, I looked around at the girls gathered at the table. Lynn, the one who had arrived only a week before, was still insisting on her Gothic look. Sophie noted to me earlier that new girls tried to hang onto makeup and styled hair for a few weeks and then gave up. Looking at Lynn, I was reminded of the bumper sticker I had seen on a car in Bend driven by a girl with black lips, spiked black hair, and black clothes. "I am so Gothic that when I look in the mirror there is no reflection," it said. It was flaunted on the dented fender as though it were a position of rebellion. Instead it seemed a statement of all that was not right with the driver: she couldn't see herself, didn't exist for herself. Lynn was pierced, eyebrow, lip, tongue. Tattoos circled her upper arms. She was beautiful and funny and smart. She was adopted, lived outside of Phoenix with her father, a doctor, and her mother, a teacher. She had two siblings, the biological children of her adoptive family. All had gone well until her early teens, and then she imploded. "Melt down," as Sophie called it. Lynn became unable to receive love, to accommodate the notion that she was loved, or belonged anywhere. She was one of three adopted girls at Fay's, all suffering from attachment disorder, apparently increasingly common among adopted children, according to Fay, who explained that some take terrible measures to try and jolt themselves out of their state of dislocation or to confirm it—self-mutilation, fouling their environment. I wondered to what extent all of us who have experienced trauma are suffering from an attachment disorder, unable to subscribe to the notion we are wanted and loved, belong, are seen. Because we feel none of that for ourselves, we are unable to detach from a sense of being in free fall, disassociated. When we stand in front of a mirror, we see nothing reflected there.

Brilliant in its common sense, Fay's approach was not to change Lynn's style of dress, or her taste in music, but to let Lynn feed sheep and slop hogs dressed in her long black capes with carefully manicured black finger nails and black lips, earphones tight to her head blasting metallic lyrics about death and destruction. Fay's husband had the same offhanded way, asking Lynn to help with loading bales of hay to feed the cattle and Lynn having to maneuver her unusual choice of clothing around the task until eventually, Sophie later told me, she discarded some of her Gothic image because it was no longer practical. Not because anyone said it wasn't OK, but because, when she stood in front of the mirror, she gradually began to see herself, to see her own reflection, and relinquish the need for masks and costumes.

Lynn's Gothic style caused a stir in the tiny town of Bow when Fay brought her along with the other girls to take in a local basketball game or community pot luck. For the most part, the community took a wait-and-see attitude about Fay's start-up program, reserving judgment about something they didn't entirely understand. But others spread false stories and the girls knew their reconstructed confidence would be put to the test as they increasingly sought to blend in with the community.

I fell asleep to whispered debates between the girls on the third floor about whose turn it was to get up and feed the piglets their bottle. My accommodations were improvisational, a bed in a room awaiting the rest of its furnishings. But the view was first class, out the window toward the Milk River, to the stand of cottonwoods, and through them to a glimpse of eternity. I recalled my rancher friend who reminded me that ranchers don't ranch for the money, but for the psychic income. I was cashing in this night. I fell asleep with the window wide open to the sounds of a trace of wind that had lost its steam traveling the miles across the prairie, the whistle of night hawks, the rustling of livestock in the underbrush.

Well before the sun was up, my sleep was distracted by the sound of hooves running back and forth, back and forth nervously, then frantically. It seemed a dream at first, the sound, something I dimly recalled having heard before. I struggled to remember where I was—what bed, what room, what place. A short, swift bark and then again—the panicked patter of hooves. I suddenly sat upright in bed. I knew, I knew absolutely. Dogs were running the sheep. A death sentence. No wound need be inflicted. Sheep eerily will keel over simply from the stress of being run. I pulled pants on over my pajamas and ran to wake Fay whose bedroom was on the other side of the house. We both tore outside and, positioning ourselves between the dogs and the terrified sheep, ran the dogs off. She then walked through the sheep, taking inventory. Her gratitude, needless to say, was enormous. None of the sheep had succumbed, none were injured. But more important to me was the reassurance that those sounds prompted an automatic response from me, even twelve years removed from ranching. Over the course of two decades living on the desert, I watched my own instincts, my own cellular knowledge of things blossom. My hearing, my sight, my sense of touch all became more acute. I am convinced as humans we spend our time silting over our instinctual potential, silencing our innate skills as forager, survivor, as mother. I hadn't completely forgotten.

After breakfast, Sophie drove me to the school house that had become the academic headquarters for Fay's girls and where Sophie went to school every day. Rayleen and Hazel were there. It was like meeting them for the first time. In sharp contrast to our first encounter, I was now able to see them as the committed, bright, and creative women they were, daily helping my daughter piece her academic and emotional life back together, readying her for entry into the local school system. The building had all the vintage charm of western one-room schoolhouses—white clapboard siding with a small belfry, three tall, rectangular windows down each side, and a tall entry door with smaller windows on each side. It sat on the edge of a dirt road, overshadowed by cottonwoods that drank liberally from the Milk River flowing behind the school. Inside it had the familiar smell of a place with a long-standing relationship with books and ink and paints. Rayleen was finishing grading some papers. She welcomed me and we talked, with Sophie willingly there, of the progress being made and where work was needed, of their efforts to consolidate the credits from Bend so they matched the Montana requirements for her year and grade, their research into various correspondence programs to find the best English literature and Algebra II courses. I felt immediately comforted and on familiar ground talking about measurables like grades and course credits. In my mind's eye, I had already taken and developed a finished photo of Sophie at Bow High School and was on to the next image I needed for my family album, offering only superficial acknowledgment of what Sophie had accomplished to date: "Sophie, this is great. You are such a good student! So what are your thoughts about college? This is the time to start thinking about it, you know—in terms of outside activities and things." My first visit in three and one half months, Sophie having only just begun the process of sheeting in the wildly flapping sails of her life, and I am asking her about college plans! My question inspired shocked silence in Rayleen and Hazel. I had listened only to the dictates of my own need to impose an order I was familiar with. I instantly felt the sting of regret at my comment and awkwardly apologized to Sophie. I couldn't tell if she heard me. The good news was that the lag time between acting out of my own lostness, and realizing it, was shrinking.

Rayleen gingerly returned to the topic of high school credits. "It is looking good for Sophie and she is working hard. I see no reason, if she mainstreams into our high school next semester and completes another literature correspondence course this summer, that she won't be set for junior year wherever she decides to go to high school next fall."

I was supposed to be ready for this, the question of next year. In our one-on-one conference earlier that morning, Fay had mentioned my need to address the issue with Sophie, had coached me on the subject, urging me to stand my ground, state whatever I felt in my heart would be best for Sophie and see what happened, to practice letting go of the fear that my children would go away from me if I said and did what I felt they needed, to trust my instincts.

"What should I say, Fay?" I pleaded.

"What do you feel?" her rejoinder. And here it was, laid out on the table, the question of next steps, what school, how long to stay at Northern Lights. I took in a breath.

"The plan," I announced with more resolve than I was used to hearing from me, the decision more ripened than I was aware of, "is to complete junior year here." I did it. I said it. Sophie would still be underage until the following July. I was, in theory, still in charge.

"Mam, no *way*. I'm not going to Bow High School! I'm coming back to Bend!"

"We can talk about it, Sophie," I deflected, feeling my own fears resurfacing.

"There's plenty of time, Sophie," reassured Rayleen. "It's only March."

The last stop on our tour was the site, at the foot of the Bear Paw Mountains, where Chief Joseph surrendered after a year-long retreat from northeastern Oregon. His people exhausted, starving, and cold, he would "fight no more forever." Sophie had what it took to break the awkward silence between us to tell me she had come here once or twice on her own and wanted to show me. We walked through the breathlessness of the space gentled by a carpet of soft prairie grasses, over the ground where members of Joseph's brave band had fallen to musket fire, signified by round, quarter-sized pewter disks, dramatic in their understated simplicity, pounded into the ground with their names inscribed—mighty names. Names that invoked bears and eagles, sun and moon, wind and fire, bravery and wisdom. Small prayer ties, tobacco pouches, faded red, yellow, blue, black—the colors signifying the power derived from the points on the compass—had been left on the ground by those who had come to honor their fallen ancestors and to ask for healing and strength in their own lives. The Native belief is once an elder dies, crosses over to the other side, they are available to us on earth, in wholeness, in purity, to guide us. "I love it here," Sophie said, already forgetting her false allegiance to returning to Bend. "You're lucky to have found each other," I replied, praying silently that the entire band of Joseph's people would gather on Sophie's shoulder and whisper their good counsel in her ear, and when they were done that they would come find me.

On our last evening together Sophie and I unloaded the box of photography supplies. We entertained ourselves with ideas of how to convert the basement bathroom in the big green house into a darkroom, together recalling earlier forays into the magic of photography in the feedlot scale house. But the retreat into the darkroom wouldn't happen now, I could tell. She wanted the option, wanted the tools accessible to her, but wasn't quite ready. First she had to develop confidence that she could trust this place, that she could express anger or resentment, could store enough love of herself that she had some to genuinely offer others—four legged and two—and that this expansive place, as abundant, and real, and secure as Fay's hugs, wouldn't go away in the process. She needed to stake practical claim to herself and her surroundings before she would be ready to go into the darkroom to begin to expose the hazy images of past trauma, to develop the clearly delineated portraits of a young woman returning to herself.

TEN

Wedding Party

My niece announced that she planned to get married in early June, six months following Sophie's arrival in Bow. I seized on the chance. Somewhere for all of us to be together, as a family, that wasn't Bend. I was not ready for Sophie to come back to Bend, even for a short visit. I wanted to postpone the inevitable as long as I could.

The wedding was to be held in South Carolina. Stephen, Isabelle, Nick, and I rendezvoused with Sophie in the Minneapolis airport and then flew on together from there. We had enough time on a layover in Houston to buy a dress and sandals for Sophie to wear to the wedding, as well as tennis clothes for all of us for a family tournament, part of the bridal festivities. Nick and Isabelle never left Sophie's side as she wandered dazed through the racks of clothes, past jewelry glittering inside glass cases. They were like battle-weary soldiers briefly reunited while on leave in a strange port, recognizing in each other their shared experience of war. They didn't know why they were there and, except for the chance to see one another, wished they weren't. I pressed on, gathering up enough white, pleated tennis skirts, shorts, and socks with pom-poms on the heels for all of us. What a colossal joke. As though by whitewashing each of us, we would become WASP white bread, be what we appeared, not what we were. In our tennis outfits, we would become the exemplar nuclear family on the court, laughing and playing masterfully, being good sports, and engaging with the other family members, eating cucumber sandwiches with the crusts trimmed off, sipping iced tea courtside and shouting "Good shot!" at the appropriate times.

The children endured the well-intended questions that had nothing to do with their reality. Questions about what each of them were "up to," where they were in school, what were their summer travel plans, how was great aunt so and so. "How's that Dad of yours? Still ranching?" thinking they were being kind to include reference to him. People we hadn't seen in years, if ever. People who had no idea. Each of us cooperated by denying our story to ourselves in order to survive the tiny, prickly inquisitions leveled by women in pistachio-colored dresses with straw bags over one arm and wide-brimmed hats with fake flowers on the side, with lipstick that feathered along the thin, telltale creases beyond the boundaries of their lips. Or by men in pale suits, brightly colored ties, and shirts with collars pinned down with small brass clips, their initials woven carefully into the cuff of their sleeves. They wanted to know what sports the children played and who was the man I was with, what did he do, where in the East was he from, where did he do his graduate work. I wasn't as quick as my friend Irv, a Montana cowboy, who, when in England, was asked by a stuffy, matronly English woman if he had attended Eton. His reply to his befuddled inquisitor: "No, but I am fixin' to."

When none of our answers provided any familiar landmarks, didn't allow them to connect the dots from prep school to Ivy League college, the questioning trailed off and conversation ceased. And though I knew I could salvage things by playing the game of who do you know, I had no energy for it and we redirected our attention to the tennis match and the crustless sandwiches cut into triangles.

The event was held at a "destination" resort. As though other places we go aren't destinations, or as though once we get to this resort we have "arrived." Perfect lawns, no trash, no decisions, no issues, no news to fill even a postcard. People eased their cars over the white-striped speed bumps, past houses facing manmade ponds that, I imagined, glowed in the dark for all the fertilizer that washed into their propylene-lined shores. Small golf carts transported gray-haired people in bright madras plaid jackets or capri pants. If I took many more hits in my life, maybe I'd come to understand this concept of premature burial, this placid, glassy life with no white caps.

Meanwhile, behind this scene of calm and resort and destination, an insidious subplot was brewing, for, as I later learned, Sophie had made contact with her father. He had hatched a plan "to bust her." She would sneak back to our hotel suite, she revealed months afterward, and make secret calls to him to work out the details. The plan was he would meet her during the layover in Minneapolis. She would pretend to go to the restroom, but instead would find him at his gate and together they would head for freedom. She cupped her hands over the phone, turning her back when I came in or when the maid came to collect dirty towels or when Stephen came bounding in to retrieve a forgotten tennis racket.

"Who is on the phone?" I asked.

"What is this, Twenty Questions? Can't I even call my friends?" she fired back.

It was her first trip away from Montana. Her first exposure to us as a family and in a completely strange setting. She seemed to need to get in touch with something, someone that felt familiar, even if it was not good for her. Her brother and sister knew about the plan, and though on their own had been showing encouraging signs of separating themselves from his influence, when reunited as a group immediately became accomplices, saying nothing. They resubscribed to his secret society, not realizing they plotted against themselves and their own right to happiness by enlisting in his demented army. This was their father, after all. They were doing what he said. His power to play them off each other, to enroll them in his plot, was formidable. Sophie's hope was that maybe this time, as perilous as the plan sounded, as threatening to her safety as it would be, he would follow through, do what he had said he would do. Just this once.

We didn't connect in any idealized way as a family, what there was left of it, but we did share oxygen and toothpaste. We did feel the brush of our arm against the other. We did break bread together. And sadly, we did resume our customary roles: mother as crusader, father as predator, children as skiffs on a troubled sea.

The wedding ceremony itself was held in a church perched on the edge of a saltwater marsh. The trees wept with moss. The air was thick and languid. Men lounged like bolts of black velvet against brightly colored cars at corner 7-Elevens enveloped by magnolias. Vast mansions and cotton farms. Elaborate gardens and Bel Epoch architecture. We assembled at the doorway of the small, white church. One by one, we were shown in. For some reason, all my siblings were seated in the pews that flanked the altar, next to one another. There was no room for me. It was an oversight. No biggy. But for me every old emotion of being the youngest, forgotten, left behind, crowded to the surface. I no longer saw the tidy wooden pews with the needle-pointed knee cushions placed precisely at each place, the white walls, the mullioned windows like see-through steeples. No longer smelled the sachet of the women entering or the abundance of flowers arranged in the front of the church. I was oblivious to all but my own falling, like Alice in Wonderland, down, down, down the rabbit hole of a message indelibly imprinted on my view of things, sense of self. The sequence of cues so perfectly orchestrated—one by one, all but me, in a place of honor. I was unable to redirect the emotion, to be a grown up. In the presence of our families of origin it is impressive how quickly we fall into old patterns and roles. I doubt any of my siblings realized my anguish. It was the normal sequence of events for them too. I simultaneously saw my neediness and the ludicrousness of my response. I managed to whisper to Stephen that I was experiencing an emotional nosedive, all passengers advised to lean forward in their seats. I pressed my forehead against the back of the pine pew. "Dear God, if this could have such an impact on me, what might a return to Bend have on Sophie? I pray she doesn't come home any time soon."

To get to the reception after the wedding ceremony we walked down a lane that opened up to the marsh and beyond it, the fish-scale gray Atlantic Ocean. The lane was thickly banked on either side by dense growth—fragrant bougainvillea, honeysuckle, spicy pink-petaled rugosa roses. The building that housed the reception was a low, long building with a wooden shingled roof spanning the wide porches all around. All of us walked there slowly, following bagpipers who led the postceremonial processional. There was a surreal quality to the whispered exchanges, the slow-motion walk, chintz skirts swaying back and forth, the women's arms making a triangle shape from shoulder to head, like delicate flying buttresses, securing their hats as they walked into the sea breeze.

After we went through the receiving line, the band started playing. My brother immediately got up to dance, first with his wife and then with each of his daughters. Other fathers did the same. Soon my brother came and asked Isabelle. She looked up at him and, suddenly overcome with tears, rushed off to the bathroom. Sophie coldly declined. They had been simultaneously scorched by the realization that there would be no father to dance at their weddings. What could they hope for?

I had attended a small, all-girl Episcopal boarding school in northern New Hampshire. Once a year a father–daughter dance was held. The fathers would arrive on Friday night for dinner. The next day they watched their daughters play field hockey. Our art was on display in the hallway of the main building. Portfolios of our work in Latin, French, algebra, biology, and history were fanned out across tables in each classroom. Teachers were on hand to discuss our status as a student. Saturday night was the dance. My father was a handsome man and a good dancer. I was so proud to have him as my dance partner. I was so proud to have him as a father. I adored him. He was brilliant, not only by my standards, but by anyone's. He was debonair, gentle, and kind. I put my arm through his as we walked out on to the dance floor. I knew I had a father, as reliably as the floor was under my feet. I had written "Dad" across both tiny pages of the dance card tied tight with ribbon around my wrist.

At the Minneapolis airport on our return, Sophie was nervous, preoccupied, darting in and out of the women's room, making frantic calls on the pay phone, scanning each long concourse. She was, as it turned out, looking for a father who wasn't there, never would be. Mustering an encouraging smile, I waved Sophie on to the connecting flight back to Northern Lights.

ELEVEN

Egg Run

"What would you think about going to visit Sophie in Montana," I proposed to Isabelle and Nick when they both were at home on the same day. They were skeptical. The wedding trip, less than a month before, had hardly been anyone's idea of fun. "The end of July," I proposed. They were leery. They didn't want to give the impression they supported what I had done. Sending Sophie to Northern Lights a good thing, a necessary thing? Never. My guess was they wanted their family to appear normal, not have outrageous fathers, controlling mothers, not have acting-out siblings, not be reminded they had addiction issues of their own, wished my actions wouldn't call attention to how different our family was. I knew about this. Those who assumed Sophie was still away at the college preparatory school in Portland—I didn't tell them differently. Or if they did ask me where she was, I simply replied: "In Montana." "In school?" I nodded yes. And when they assumed college, I didn't tell them differently. I excused it as a way of protecting Sophie. In fact, it was the headline I liked, I wanted.

Having been sent to Trek West himself, Nick felt that at any moment I might interrupt his life again. He didn't trust me, worried that hanging around me too long was dangerous. I explained the trip would let them see Northern Lights, draw their own conclusions, and that I felt we needed to witness and support Sophie as a family. What I was thinking as I was saying this was that there were issues we needed to address as a group. The only way for all of us to transcend them was to exorcise the demons that were bossing us around. To dig them out, rout them out. But if I had said this to Isabelle and Nick, they would never have come. I wanted to go fast, get it done, so life, the life I wanted for them and for me, could begin. What was because of me? Bring it on. I was ready, or so I thought. What was because of their father? Well, then say so. What was dictating their actions still? My sense was that life wasn't happening, wouldn't start for my children or me until this task was accomplished, so let's get on with it. Fay, work your magic. Heal us, each of us, in two days. Heal us. I will bring my children to you, to the waters of the Milk River.

They eventually agreed. Nick said he was willing to go, with the caveat that "no one was going to shrink his head." He was going because, "dude, he wanted to see Sophie." Isabelle's jaw set as she reluctantly nodded her acceptance of the plan, preparing to defend her defendedness, to battle anyone who threatened to huff and puff too hard on her delicate emotional construct, carefully designed to keep the wolf at bay. I called Fay.

"The whole lot of you! I'll reserve the weekend."

Nothing makes me hum like all of us together and away. A family unit, a sense of wholeness engendered by being linked by an away place. South Carolina missed the mark. Maybe this trip would be different. Maybe this trip would be more like the annual summer trips with the children to the East Coast, all of us seated next to one another on the airplane. Suspended in time and space, as though flying above the clouds at 30,000 feet gave me permission to believe whatever I wanted about this small band and our future together. Any story I could tell myself would hold true until we landed and were thrust back into the act and scene of real time. Like lying in the bath tub as the water slowly drains, my naked body reluctantly returning to weightedness, to the world of gravity. Every summer in anticipation of the flight East I would make small care packages for the trip that the children couldn't open until we reached altitude—coloring books, small tinker toys to drive along the edges of the folding tray table. No rewards in life until you reach altitude.

Once we got to Cape Cod, Isabelle, Nick, and Sophie walked the same lane to the beach I walked as a child, scurrying ahead, their inflated floaties jutting their arms out to the side like odd, flightless insects; their big and middle toes ill-accustomed to the thong of their sandals, producing a lopsided gait; striped beach towels sagging off their skinny summer shoulders. They slid down the banister of the old house, bare feet setting up a cadence against the railings like a stick along a picket fence, chased fireflies into the pitch of the dense undergrowth on summer nights. The sentence of our oneness was perfectly punctuated. There was no harm done. Amazing I didn't cluck out loud so overwhelming was my contentment, my sense of security in having them corralled with me inside a defined place, happily hosted by a defined piece of time.

For years while ranching in the desert I had an egg run. I gathered the eggs, wiped off bits of chicken manure and stuck feathers, and placed them—brown and warm and oval—into the egg cartons I saved in a dusty pile on top of the refrigerator. I then loaded them into a large box padded with old newspapers and drove them forty miles of dirt road to the small general store where they were offered for sale. We had a wide assortment of chickens: Bantams, Aracana, Rhode Island Reds, Polish Leghorns. In a column I titled "Upper Country News," which I wrote for a regional weekly newspaper, I once reported it had gotten so cold one of my prized roosters had frozen to the roost. The joke went around that my husband's cock froze. Each winter he and I would delight in pouring over the catalog of exotic chickens we could and did order. The mailman, who delivered mail to us three days a week, would bring the chicks to us each spring in the back of his van. They had come by air, generally from the Midwest, enduring at least two flight changes, delivery to the nearest post office, and finally, the long drive to the ranch. A miracle any survived, many were by now hungry and cold. Some lay listlessly on their sides in the box. I would set the oven on warm and lay the toppled ones on cookie sheets, placing them gently inside the oven. Slowly, like the sweetest little popcorns, the gentle crescendo of peeps would begin as the warm temperature revived them. I would then pull them out of the oven and install them under the warming lights set up in the chicken coop, along with water and food. They were called exotics to explain the feathers that cascaded down their legs like cashmere chaps, or flamboyant plumage that arced off their tiny red eyes, like the most elaborate eyeglasses Lucille Ball could ever imagine. They laid green, khaki, and turquoise-colored eggs, which always provoked a comment when added to the brown dozens I would collect for the general store. I adored my chickens. I loved to watch them prune and peck, stretch and scratch, regard me disdainfully with their beady eye as I would reach my hand slowly under their warmth for an egg.

Summer evenings on the ranch, cultural eons from the fireflies at Cape Cod, we gathered neighbors for friendly jousts of team roping in the arena we had built by the house. They drove long dirt miles, horse trailer in tow, bringing picnics and beer. We set up a playpen at the end of the arena and put the smaller babies there. Other children played outside the roping arena under the watchful eye of the mother assigned to the rotation—much as one mother cow will stay behind with a brood of calves while the others go to water. Each team of ropers would get one steer. The header roped first, casting his loop out over the horns, and then simultaneously turning his horse and dallying his rope around the saddle horn so the saddle took the impact of stopping the speed of the racing steer. Once the horns were snagged, the header pulled the steer across the arena so the heeler could set a trap with his loop, pitching his rope in such a way that the open circle landed just in front of the steer's two hind feet. In the split second the steer stepped forward, the heeler jerked his rope upward to catch both hind feet, and dallied his rope around the saddle horn. The moment the steer was roped, head and heels, and the header turned his horse to face the heeler, the stopwatch was stopped. Most women, myself included, only heeled. There was less risk, as you were roping at a slower speed than the header. For two former Bostonians, my husband and I were a good team. We even won some of the jackpots. High stakes: a dollar a round, winning team takes all. He rarely missed. He was good at everything and always seemed to know what he was doing and why. At least he always gave that impression.

After the last horse trailer had disappeared over the hill, its dusty farewell settling on the evening, I would bathe my sleepy children in the enamel bath tub that stood on claw feet, put them in their pajamas, and tuck them into their beds, reciting prayers, reading a story. I felt such a surge of contentment and well-being as I looked out Isabelle's bedroom window, seeing no evidence of man for as far as I could see, with the exception of the dirt road that had led our guests up out of the valley we called home. We were the inventors of a life in a place so magnificent I knew nothing would upset it.

I had found a print at an art gallery in town, a prayerful rendering of my dream for our life. I gave it to my husband for his birthday that year. It showed a landscape, Japanese in its execution, of a field and then a mountain. Nothing was drawn to perspective. There were tiny houses, over-sized chickens and cows, small threads of rivers, oddly etched clouds—but the impression was one of a fairytale and a magic place. Flying over the mountain was a man and a woman, her hair streaming behind. They were holding hands as they flew. This is what I saw we had on team-roping nights like this. I would tiptoe back in to let the love I felt spill over onto my sleeping children. I would stroke the brow of sleeping Nick, tuck the covers around his animals. I would check on Isabelle and sure enough she was snuggled, thumb in mouth, with her blanket under her nose and wrapped over her hand. I would stroke the swelling egg shape of my stomach as the miracle of Sophie formed inside me.

My husband and I got to bed long after the chickens had roosted, their upright sleep only interrupted by an occasional meditative cluck, as though experiencing some sort of poultry nightmare. Until that one night when my chickens set up a racket of guttural, desperate screams and squawks. I woke my husband, begged him to go see what the matter was. "Oh, Christ!" he yelled in an angry tone full of beery disdain for what a flatfoot I was. Throwing off the covers he ran outside and grabbed the high-powered rifle that rested in a rack hung across his pickup's rear window. The raccoon that had feasted on my chickens had long since fled. The hens staggered in crazed circles, their heads bobbing off to one side, blood jetting out of their necks. He started shooting into the dark near the chicken coop. I thought he knew what he was doing. Then wildly, madly, in every direction: at the barn, into the night sky, at the shadow of the pickup reflected on the hard dirt circle under the yard light. A shot penetrated our bedroom wall and went through our mattress. Another I didn't discover until next morning tore through the wall of Isabelle's room where she slept. I dared not consider what might have happened nor what had possessed the man who had done this. After all, he knew what he was doing. He always gave that impression. He came back in and stood in the bedroom doorway, grinning, puckish, his shadow looming over me in the bed like a giant raptor.

"Damn! I missed!"

The next night when the raccoon returned, I went, hands shaking, out into the dark with a flashlight. "You know what to do," he yelled out the bedroom window.

"I *don't* know," I muttered.

"Figure it out or you're gonna have a lot of dead chickens. There's a pistol on the wheel if you don't want to try your luck with the rifle. Maybe you'll miss the house." Laughing, he slammed the window shut.

Emboldened by the sight of my mangled hens, I gingerly took the pistol from the holster lashed to the truck's steering column and aimed the flashlight toward the chicken coop. There he was. The raccoon stood up on his hind legs and looked straight at me, the flashlight eerily illuminating his red eyes. He swayed slightly to get a better look, smell—his mouth in a slight smile, his eyes masked in black, his paws covered with blood that he nervously licked every so often. I don't know how long we stared at each other. Neither of us moved. I wondered if my eyes glowed red. I slowly raised the pistol in one hand, keeping the flashlight trained on the raccoon with the other. For the first time in my life I shot a living thing. He crumpled into a small, bleeding pile of fur. My hands shook. I looked toward the house. The windows were dark. When would I reach altitude?

By far my favorite chickens were my Bantam hens, stalwart, fearless. And what mothers! When a hawk circled over, casting the shadow so boldly imprinted on their tiny chicken brains, it set off a reflex alarm, shrill and certain. They whistled up their tiny babies, smaller than baby quail, and somehow managed to tuck them all under their small, round bodies, the tiny chicks peeking out from under their mothers' feathery breasts. The hens sat, like squat queens wearing awkward hoop skirts, cocking their heads this way and that, rolling their tiny eyes skyward to make sure all danger had passed. When I had the children to myself during our summer visits to Cape Cod I felt utterly content. No need to whistle them in close. Here we could run free, no predators, disguised as fathers, hovered. I didn't know there was another place where all of us could feel this safe, but there was.

Bow was hot and dry the July we visited Sophie. The immensity of the space silenced Isabelle and Nick. Though they thought they knew about such things growing up on the High Desert ranch, they hadn't experienced northern Montana's version. Oregon's sage-covered outback seemed intimate next to the air and space that Montana claimed as its own. The Milk River ran brown, ran thin and low along the gumbo flats that summer. The insatiable demands for irrigation water, and the end of the snow melt off the Bear Paws, was scored on the drying and cracked clay banks. The sheep gathered panting under the cottonwoods waiting out the hot spell. The place itself appeared leached and ramshackle. The piles of old rusted vehicles were still there. The chicken coop still leaned into the slight shrug of the ground. Sheets luffed gently from a line strung between the cistern and the corner of the house and as they sleepily lifted, revealed a view of unending yellowed grasslands extending all the way to Canada.

Despite their guardedness, Fay, in her cutoffs and irrigating boots, her long hair pulled back and secured by a chop stick and wearing a faded T-shirt that said Kiss Me, worked her magic on Isabelle and Nick within minutes of their arrival. She gave Isabelle a task in the kitchen that she could take refuge in and from which safe vantage point she could get her bearings. She asked Nick how the surgery went on his shoulder, could she have a look? Before he knew it, Nick had his shirt halfway over his head as Fay carefully examined the row of stitches. By the end of the weekend, each of us had "counseled" with her, first one on one, then the three of them without me. All of us, it seemed, had found a place as safe as Cape Cod, had found solace nestled under Fay's protective wings.

One of the other programs I had considered for Sophie held regularly scheduled regional meetings for the parents, putting them through the same step program their children were experiencing, with the idea that when their child returned home, the parents would have some of the skill set taught their child. Fay's approach was anything but that. Any skill set she was teaching Sophie was not systematic, instead was Sophie-directed—based on Sophie's willingness and readiness to "hear," to "learn." There was no lesson plan, this week dealing with father issues, next, mother issues, followed by abandonment, addiction, self-esteem. No, they were all rolled up into a tangled heap, the unraveling to be done carefully, slowly by Sophie, who, as though playing the spider-web game at a child's birthday party, followed her colored strand of yarn to the prize of finding herself, undoing the snarls as she came upon them. It wasn't that a process wasn't underway, it was just that Fay's approach couldn't, as far as I could see, be mapped, plotted. The only complementary skill set I could develop was to learn to patiently undo my knots as I followed my own strand that looped and spiraled in and around my children's.

The final meeting with Fay, the family session, involved us all. I felt optimistic about how it would go, proud of how united and caring we seemed to be. Fay had prepared me, stating Isabelle, Nick, and Sophie needed to be allowed to express their anger at the fact that I hadn't been able to make the hurt go away. She coached me to listen, to let them speak their piece.

We gathered in the front room, Fay and Nick in the large easy chairs and Isabelle, Sophie, and I sharing the sofa in front of the window that framed the steady, unwavering gaze of land and sky. I began the meeting sitting on the edge of the couch, my back straight, at the ready, in charge. Fay led off, speaking to me as she told me she would. "What I am hearing from Sophie is that her root experience is emotional abandonment at a very early age, by her father, yes, but also by you, Ellen. She saw your fear, how it dominated you. She concluded you had all you could handle, and she was one too many, that she was unwelcome." I tried not to hear Nick and Isabelle acknowledging they saw themselves in that description. But Fay heard them and continued: "After what you have all been through, it's hard to move forward into new experiences, to trust there is goodness, to fill the void created by this sense of internal homelessness."

I wasn't able to maintain my straight-backed posture of composure and self-control on the edge of the sofa for long. Fay's preamble opened the flood gates. The rapid fire that ensued threw me up against the ropes, robbed me of the stories I told myself about how well I had managed them, and our shared circumstances. I slumped back against the cushions. Isabelle stated icily that she had raised herself. Sophie tearfully said so had she. Nick nodded. I felt socked in the ribs. My best was not enough. My feathery skirts proved scant protection. I rose ferociously to my defense. "You want to see what raising yourself looks like? I'll tell you about raising yourself," I blurted, and cited all the things I had done: good schools, a roof over their heads, clothes, dentists, doctors, summer camps, trips East, hot meals. "Mam," said Sophie, "I just wanted more hugs, more down time." Keeping them from their father hadn't worked, they said. *Were they shouting?* "We love Dad. He's our father, don't you get it?" I had made things worse, *it sounded like screaming*, by not giving them any means to reconcile the two realities of their lives, and I was supposed to be the one in charge! They accused me of making it even harder by rejecting him and therefore rejecting them. The madness, the disconnect they experienced in *both* parents drove them underground. They had needed my companionship and compassion, not fixing.

Most of all they hated me, *I think they used that word: "hate,"* for my embarrassment about them, about him, about me.

I couldn't handle it. It felt like mother bashing. Though I dimly recalled Fay's advice to let them vent, to let their words flow over me, I got caught in the boil, couldn't keep any distance from the emotions that welled inside of me. I raged and then sobbed—primal, spastic. Isabelle responded with anger, demanded I shape up. Nick numbed out: "What did you say?" Sophie cried, pleading with me to stop crying. I finally got to a place of emotional nakedness and surrender. I remembered what Fay had said to me that morning. "We can avoid reality by living unconsciously. But when we do we are bound to remain authors of our own despair." I had assumed then it was about Sophie. I looked over at my three children. I thought I knew what they had been through, but I realized I had no notion, not really. I could think of nothing to say or do about what I had heard. I was out of ideas, on my knees to the enormity of their experience and their exclusive ownership of it. I saw the folly and sheer audacity of my trying to protect them from their own lives. Perhaps, I thought, all each of us can do is find the combination to our hearts. And most of the time we can only work the lock from the inside.

They saw the softening, the yielding expressed in my face, my body, and, perhaps for the first time, caught a glimpse of the essence of me: full of love, full of imperfections. We rose in unison, levitated by the power of our emotions. We embraced silently, and, leaving the damp piles of Kleenex on the sofa and chairs, walked out of the room, the four of us, shoulder to shoulder, out into the scorching sun, scattering the chickens as we went down the gumbo driveway, the Milk River bounding us on one side, the straight stretch of highway on the other, the panting sheep, the sleeping dogs, the fields of barley, the pigs and garden and cows and trucks and piles of junk metal. We walked out across the high plains toward the Bear Paw Mountains until we were just four small dots on the flat horizon, changing the profile of the earth for as long as we went.

TWELVE

Homecomings

Relapse is part of recovery. That's what Fay had said to prepare me for Sophie's first trip back to Bend since going to Northern Lights. I couldn't think of anymore detours and distractions. I couldn't put it off any longer. Sophie would come for two weeks in August, a break at home before her junior year started at the Bow High School. *"Relapse and recovery. . . . R and R drug rehab style,"* I mused. Sophie wanted to work out some final details about transferring credits, and to salvage the car her father had given her, bring it to Bend and park it at my house. She had abandoned it at the ranch months before. On this trip Sophie would also see Megan and Rachel for the first time in nearly a year. And then, back to Montana.

Fay helped me accept the fact that short trips home were important. Sophie had to see what tools she could put to use from her new kit. I was terrified of a relapse, so afraid she wouldn't want, and I wouldn't be able, to persuade her to go back to Bow. If I put my foot down, I worried out loud to Fay, she might run away or do something that would harm her. Fay acknowledged, in a tone reserved for those who have stated the obvious, that any of this might happen, and that is why the trips home were important. Sophie was still under eighteen. We still had some recourse. Sophie developing a false sense of recovery in a vacuum was ultimately of no use, Fay said. She needed to take short visits back to the very place that was so loaded, so toxic—like putting a plant out to harden, a little bit at a time. After a few stumbles, Fay felt, Sophie would adapt and be able to handle Bend on her own, could learn to survive exposure to her friends still stuck in their old patterns, to her father. And, Fay included, to me, her mother who was unwilling to hold her daughter accountable; a mother afraid of the possibility of things needing to spin out of control again and, maybe, again, before and in order to find center; a mother who repeatedly engaged in her own form of relapse, falling back into the cold embrace of fear, shame, and indecisiveness; a mother seduced by her version of the story, unable to accept what was. She had me pegged.

In Oregon's High Desert country, ranchers turn out all but a couple of horses during the winter. Mother cows are wintered close-in to be fed and, come spring, to calve, so for at least three months or so there's no need for horse power. Out in the hills, horses scavenge what sparse winter feed they can, bolstered by protein blocks or a bale of sweet timothy hay left for them every so often. When the time comes for spring branding and turning cattle out on to summer pasture, the cavvy of horses are rounded up, often using a rope corral. It's nothing more than a long, thick braid of nylon rope suspended between steel fence posts driven haphazardly into the ground for the occasion, the suggestion of a circle. But because everything about what those cowboys describe in sound and motion—calm, steady, confident—says fence, not rope, says solid, not flimsy, the horses buy into the concept. They circle inside the flimsy hold, ears forward, round and round like it was built of massive rock, like it was impenetrable.

At the start of Sophie's stay I built a rope corral of my expectations of her. I acknowledged the challenges this first trip home presented, but told her nevertheless I expected she would respect me and my concerns for her by letting me know where she was at all times. I didn't say: "Any evidence of drugs or alcohol and you're gone." I would have been setting myself up. Fay had coached me. "Sophie needs to make the right or wrong decisions without your voice as her conscience ringing in her ears." That was one of Fay's many remarkable skills. She never became a substitute, never allowed her girls to adopt her as their scapegoat. I had the opportunity to put that into practice now. Sophie had to see if her own voice had gained strength, if she could hear her own counsel above the din of her friends. I then told Sophie if she didn't afford me that level of respect, I would put her on a flight to Montana immediately. I surprised myself. I meant it. Sophie circled inside my words, ears forward, head high, checking it out and agreed. We were off to a good start.

I was also making progress. I had gotten used to living alone and liked it. Stephen came most weekends, but otherwise I had the house to myself. I began to slough some of the scar tissue. I gradually returned to myself. I was able to register that there were people who sought my company, were glad I was on the planet. You can't overdo telling people who have had life's rug pulled out from under them how glad you are they exist. And too, one careless, hurtful statement rings in their ears like a thunder clap and sends them running for cover. But despite my novitiate status, I gradually felt more welcome in the world. Women friends wanted to go to a movie, with *me*. I joined a French club, a writing group. I began to honestly acknowledge the damage done during sixteen years of marriage, and the ten years since, single-handedly fighting the domestic war on drugs. I realized I had a role to play in the healing of my children. I now realized to do that effectively *I* had to heal, and had to take that process seriously. And while I did, I had miraculously found a place for Sophie that would nurture her, more effectively than I was able.

Sophie noticed my growing assurance. I don't think she had ever experienced it before. The more confident I became, the safer she felt. I saw this. It fueled my conversion. In the past, there had always been the telltale hiss of a small leak, a slight draft of uncertainty, of my questioning my right, ability, or commitment to enforce what I was saying. In laying out the ground rules for her visit, I still wobbled a little, but not like before, not enough to cancel the import of what I said. She acknowledged me—not with the tone of one dismissing an idle threat, an adult posturing as parent, but with a healthy testiness that disguised her respect for what I said.

I can ask this now: Where are the grown-ups? Where are the adults who are not afraid to set down rules and regulations, whether their children like it or not? We are a society dominated by the fear our children won't like us. So we hand the reins over to them, giving them so much power they are terrified. With the bit between their teeth they gallop headlong into addiction, delinquency, looking for solace and shelter. They feel unclaimed, unseen, disregarded, unloved, not cared for in ways that speak to them about their safety and well-being. They are raised in an environment that is soft in the middle. Parent as pal. Child enthroned. Infant kings and queens—who with haughty arrogance that masks their fear at feeling so unsafe, act out in ways that are more and more strident cries for predictability, consistency, rules, regulations, and the love described by those who care enough to take a stand. Parenting is not a popularity contest. We make appointments with a therapist to ask if it is OK that our child is smoking dope, sniffing glue. Is it OK that I go into my kid's room to check out my concern that my child is feeling suicidal? Where are we as a culture that we have to ask permission to parent, as though by doing the right and responsible thing we are overstepping our bounds? How has it come to this? If we are a stepping stone for our children to any destination—then we are treated accordingly. If we proselytize youth, then anyone older than young is of no value, deserves no respect.

As Sophie's stay wore on, I fought my instinct to assume the worst was happening each night she was out. "Hold her as able, hold her as able!" Fay coached me. I didn't linger within earshot when she was on the telephone or stand nervously behind the door each time she came in or headed out. Instead, I went about my business and created some opportunities for us to spend time together, like lunch out at a downtown cafe.

"How are Megan and Rachel? Did they stay in touch with you while you were gone?" I asked over soup and sandwiches.

"They stayed in touch pretty much. They are still my best friends, always will be." she answered.

"They wrote? Called?"

"Yeh. Some. Both," she replied without elaborating.

Later she would acknowledge that their interest in maintaining contact had fallen away in direct proportion to their perceived influence on her. The more she reclaimed herself, the less they had to do with her. She was no longer a member of their tribe. She had discarded the uniform of black hooded sweatshirts and blue jeans with the hems dragging in the dirt, no longer spoke their language defined by various declensions of fuck, no longer consumed the same symbolic substances—their shared communion. But they remained her friends. She was very loyal to them. The trick was to hang on to her new sense of self in the context of their expectations.

"How was it seeing them?"

"They told me I've been brainwashed. Have I been?"

How could they have seen it otherwise? A parent forcefully removes a child, and then that child, that friend of theirs, now claims to like where she is? It had to be brainwashing. To them, pulling someone out of the water before they drowned translated into pushing someone under and holding them there. Megan and Rachel saw me as the enemy. They wouldn't come in the house if I was there. They would wait in their parked car, stereo on full blast. They feared and disliked me. The feeling was mutual. I felt unable to bridge the gap, though realizing if I could it would go a long way to healing the differences Sophie and I had, help speed her process. But I couldn't, wasn't grown-up enough to. Indeed, I feared their power over Sophie in her fragile state of recovery. I resented them for tempting Sophie, in the name of friendship, with beer, cigarettes, and drugs as a means of reestablishing their influence over her.

But back to the question. Had she been brainwashed? Which time? By the unconscionable messages from her father? Yes. By the messages from the peer group she took refuge in? Yes. By her own garbled dictates to herself about herself? Yes. By her mother's lofty speeches and elaborate solutions that whitewashed the dark undercurrents running through her life? Yes. By the bravado of the Montana landscape, the heady sense of freedom it implied, the possibility of new beginnings? Yes again.

"What did you tell them when they said that?"

"I said it was bullshit. Told them I learned to like country and western music all by myself." She looked up at me with her wry smile, the one she flashed when she knew she had made a witty statement.

I hugged her. "Oh, Sophie, stay strong," and watched her go out the door to their waiting car.

━━━━━━━

Toward the last days of her stay I asked Sophie if she had figured out how to retrieve her car from her father's, a primary mission of her trip home. I didn't want her to go out there, didn't want her to see him. Of all the potential snares returning home posed, I felt contact with him would be the hardest for Sophie to avoid.

"You tell me, Mam, how else can I get my car without seeing Dad?" she said in an irritated tone. My debilitating belief that something bad was about to happen, that Sophie was weak and vulnerable and prone to poor decisions, had returned. "Act as if!" Fay's encouragement rang in my ears. As in: Sophie had made enormous strides. She would let me know what she could and couldn't handle. Like an accident victim determined to walk again—don't hover and expect the fall. Instead cheer her on.

What Sophie discovered when she went to get the car was that various of her father's druggie girlfriends had used it while she was gone, leaving it as wasted as they—dented, no front grill, smashed headlights. Her father wasn't around, though she had told him she was coming. Now the car sat in my driveway, a reminder of the tumult of Sophie's life on the run. Behind the back seat, remnants of that time: her sleeping bag, some dirty clothes, empty cigarette packages, beer cans, as though poised and waiting for her to resume her self-destructive journey.

I felt giddy, for both of us, when I saw Sophie on to the plane. I danced back to the car in the parking lot and drove home relieved, delighted we had both survived the first visit home. I had weathered her nights out, her calling from various parties, music blaring in the background. I hadn't said: "What are you doing there? Are you drinking?" I survived her toying with the idea of returning to school in Bend. I pressed the portable phone to my ear, lying in bed out of ear shot of Sophie, to be coached by Fay who reminded me just to listen. "Limit your response to 'Oh?' or 'Really?' or 'Ah hah.' Express no opinion, Ellen. The decisions are all hers. She needs to see you know how to participate with her in that way."

"Keep a deep seat and a loose rein!" cowboys will shout to a departing friend. It's also the advice offered to cowboys trying to ride a green colt. When your horse bunches up under you, ready to buck or bolt because of real or imagined surprises along the trail, don't make matters worse by tensing up, pulling in the reins, standing up in the stirrups, or you'll end up airborne for sure. Relax. Don't transmit your fear to the horse. Keep a deep seat, and a loose rein riding life's bronco.

THIRTEEN

Self and Shadow

I watched the plane climb into the air. Sophie was on her way to begin the most sober, healthy year of her life so far. Now drug free, her short-term memory had returned as had her ability to taste and enjoy food, reflected in her full and shapely figure that had replaced her emaciated appearance of almost a year earlier. She was dreaming again at night and kept a dream journal. She attended school and got good grades. She received special recognition for her writing, her art. She was on the activities committee and helped decorate the high school gym for dances, organize pep rallies. She made friends, friends who didn't drink or party, friends who were making plans for college, travel. She took a job at a local diner and at the stockyards where she and Debby, both blond and of the same energetic stature, penned cattle.

The owner of the yards was only half kidding when he said his sales had improved since the two "blondies" started penning for him. Bulls, culls, bred cows, yearling heifers, yearling steers—in and by— the two of them swinging the gates to direct the livestock into this or the other pen, down this or that alley, deftly snapping their whips of braided nylon to urge the next batch into the auction arena. The sound of the gate closing triggered the auctioneer's call: "Give me five, five, five. Do I hear five, five, five? And now seven, seven, seven? I got seven, seven, seven. And now niyen, niyen, niyen?" His voice was flat and even as the highway that led ranchers and their stock trucks and trailers to this bustling maze of pens, led them with their checkbooks and pens to this building carpeted with fresh sawdust, loose leaf tobacco stuffed into their lower lips. Layers of wooden bleachers sagged under their weight. When they spotted what they wanted, they raised an eyebrow, nodded, or barely tipped the card they held in their hand—a precise and purposeful, but practically imperceptible, gesture. Stephen had brought this report home, had seen it for himself after delivering a medical lecture in Great Falls. Still in his suit and tie, he drove four extra hours just to see Sophie run cattle into a chute.

"Hell, thought that was some some fancy damn cattle buyer you had there for us, Sophie," her boss had commented.

"No, just my mother's boyfriend."

"Damn. Pretty decent to drive this far."

"Yeh, guess it was, wasn't it?"

And I too was about to begin the most sober year of my life, sober about what was and what was not. One thing I now knew was my children couldn't learn love or compassion—or any of the things I as a parent wanted them to learn—unless I modeled it. And that did not mean doing *for* them. It meant treating myself in the manner I wanted them to treat themselves. It was a critical shift for me in my interpretation of "modeling" behavior. By sacrificing, staying up late doing laundry, spending money I didn't have to make things better—I modeled not valuing myself, not caring for myself, not being responsible to myself and my needs. By fanning the flame of their fires, I robbed them of responsibility and privilege. I got sober about what I could and could not control. I experienced the pain and exhilaration of awareness—of the impacts on all of us of my marriage, of trying to rescue three children after we had all been pitched overboard. There were things about me that increasingly couldn't be dislodged by a careless statement, by the unreasonable demands of someone else, someone else's version of who or how. I started to feel deserving of blessing, and asked to be. I accepted how blind I was during my marriage and afterward—different blind-nesses, one out of naiveté, the other out of fear, but sightless all the same. My drugs of choice started to fall away: guilt, shame, denial, dependence on codependence. I put away my white cane.

In one of many counseling sessions during this period, I spoke of the end of my marriage. So afraid of my husband at this point, I co-operated with his demands so he would not discover my plan of escape with the children. I recalled the actual, physical sensation of my spirit, my shadow-self, stepping outside of my body and allowing what took place to take place. Just to get through it. The counselor asked me to try and tell her what that shadow was saying, doing, right then, in that small room with the counselor seated in her chair opposite me on the sofa, a potted plant in the corner, the message machine blinking cries for help from others like me. I told her I could see she, yes *she,* was small, very thin, curled up, arms crossed, frail, pale skin. I stopped to take a breath.

"And is sitting there, at the opposite end of the sofa." I started to cry, shivering. I saw her so clearly. "And I can't hear a word she is saying—she keeps repeating something over and over, but she speaks so weakly, so softly. I can't hear a word."

"Soon, you will soon," the counselor reassured me.

She was right. I was retrieving this abandoned part of me. I vowed to never again be the victim of my own story. But how? There were many things I wished had not happened, but the minute I contemplated my life without those things I realized I was editing out my children, my greatest teachers. How can the story remain the same, but no longer be my captor, no longer recited in time with the dull cadence of the footsteps of the jailer? And too, how can the same story become a tool for healing, a source of strength, a chant, a cheer, a battle cry?

How? It's a question of changing tune, not story, of picking up the blunt instrument that wounded me and shaping it into something useful. For me that is this retelling. For me telling expands everything—courage, hope, the capacity to heal others. Telling stories has always had this effect, bringing healing to the raconteur and the listener. I believe our life stories are visited on us. We are somehow chosen for and by them. It remains each of our tasks to recognize our story, its lesson, and the unique means we are given to share it. Sophie and I, each in our separate ways, cautiously began to celebrate the return to who we were and could be, aligned our selves with our shadows—and started to harness the formidable power that reunion contained.

Driving home from the airport that day, I looked forward to the opportunity to reflect on Sophie's visit home and my responses to it. I was eager for the solitude of my house, a return to my schedule. But not four weeks later, Sophie was on the phone asking to come home again. It felt to me she had only just left! She and Debby, she explained, would take Amtrak to Portland and then come to Bend and together drive her car back to Montana.

Countless calls ensued between me and Debby's parents in Minnesota, each of us overwhelming our daughters with maps from the American Automobile Association, travel safety kits, instructions on changing tires and avoiding strangers. We agreed I would pick the girls up in Portland, they would stay a night or two with me, and then head back together.

The girls were deposited at the Montana train station by Fay. Forty-eight hours later, there they were, just as they said they would be, in the Portland train station. They sat waiting in the spacious, high-ceilinged, echo-y room, seated on one of the long wooden benches pocked with contemporary glyphs: initials, names, hearts, and obscenities carved into the armrests. Their knapsacks slouched at their feet on the cool Travertine marble floors. Ticket sellers peered over their spectacles at them from behind shiny brass bars. Fellow travelers moseyed about with tidy suitcases, or parcels tied with twine. On the drive to Bend, Debby and Sophie tripped over each other with tales about their overnight train ride. That morning, they recounted, they had both tried to fit into the small telephone booth-sized bathroom on the train to change clothes and clean up. These two, bursting at the seams of their new found selves, starting to get an inkling of what owning their lives felt like, stuffed themselves into the tiny W.C., and like Houdini, wriggled out of old and into new clothes, jostling for a position in front of the mirror to see what they looked like, if they were who they thought. Finally, overcome with giggles, they tumbled out of the changing room into the laps of a waiting Hutterite family sitting as still as statues, looking straight ahead, hands folded in their laps, waiting for their turn to use the lavatory, and no doubt praying for the souls of these ill-mannered, unchecked, unsupervised young women who were remembering what it was to be alive.

FOURTEEN

Hershey Kisses

By now I was convinced Sophie had proven she could survive being set out on the back porch in the cold for short periods of time. She had, it seemed to me, weathered the hardening process and could now handle Bend and any challenges it might pose.

Her next visit home would be for Christmas, with plans to go on to Debby's in Minnesota for New Year's. Debby, who had turned eighteen, had graduated from Northern Lights and returned to her hometown where she had taken an apartment of her own and was attending college. Though she and Debby had come and retrieved the car as recently as early November, this trip was different. This was Christmas. All of us reunited just like the old days: the same box of Christmas decorations, the same spot in the living room for the tree, Sharon dropping in to say hello, Stephen leaning over to stoke the fire. The same crisp cold pierced the darkness. The juniper berry wreath hung by the door, mulled wine simmered on the stove. Five stockings were hung. The mantle was covered with images of familial perfection glued to holiday greetings. It was the same promise of safety and security this scene had described a year before. It was the anniversary of Sophie being sent to Trek West.

In looking back now, I would say Sophie had keyed in on this inauspicious anniversary from the minute she arrived. I had not. So much had happened since, and weren't we all different now? Reconstructed? Didn't Sophie and I have a new relationship, on different footing? I knew this Christmas would, once and for all, confirm how back to "normal" we were.

Isabelle arrived the day after Sophie. She unpacked her special down-filled pillow, her clothes, her toothbrush and hand lotion. She scoped out the house, exclaiming about new little touches, as she was wont to do, examining who was featured in photographs magneted to the refrigerator door, making sure she was at least in some. The three of us baked cookies, painted toe nails, languished across her bed, talking nonstop about nothing in particular. She stayed that night. The next day her boyfriend showed up and she packed up and left instantly, without a trace. Sophie, who hadn't seen her on either of her previous trips to Bend, dejectedly watched her go. "Chicks before dicks," she yelled out after her, and went upstairs and slumped in front of the television, giving the Christmas tree a wide berth as though it might reach out and grab her with its branches.

Nick came by that evening. He was still playing and partying hard. Despite my asking him to support Sophie in her effort to steer clear of events that would be hard for her to handle, he instead told her about all the parties that were planned. Would she go with him, to hook up, kick it, hang, drink, cruise? Sophie looked around the living room—at the decorated tree, the garlands, candles and cards— the exact tableau that had tricked her a year before. "Yeh, Nick," she said flatly. "I'll go with you."

I watched Sophie join Nick in his Christmas sleepwalk. I watched her recoil from the ghosts of her last Christmas, recollections of being sent away. I watched her forget anything she had learned about herself since. She catapulted backward to that night and time: I was reinstated as the perpetrator of the crime, Stephen as co-conspirator. The final night of her stay, the night before she was to go to Minnesota, she was delivered to the door at 2:00 A.M., drunk. Déjà vu. I woke her up at 4:00 A.M., threw her things into her suitcase, and put her, still woozy, on her scheduled flight. What I hoped I was doing was holding Sophie as able, as responsible, as accountable for what she said she would do: spend Christmas at home and go visit Debby. It felt like an extreme act, another one.

I was gutted by her fall from grace. It had all been for nothing. We were back at square one. She was hooked, an addict. I quickly slipped into my version of the same disease. Driving home I was overcome with a longing to go home, wherever that was, where I would be welcomed, nurtured, taken care of. *I am sick of doing it all,* I wailed to myself: *bread winner, boundary setter, unconditionally loving parent. I have been robbed by drugs,* I whined, *of my husband and my relationship with my children.* I grimly realized I would forevermore be engaged in some aspect of this battle—letting go, learning to discern what was addictive behavior and what was recovery, not get my hopes up, not expect too much. I was both miserable and comforted in the company of these thoughts. How familiar they felt, how like home.

Stephen had warned if I continued to roller coaster emotionally once the children were gone, he would be forced to question staying in a relationship with me. If I did, he explained, it would mean to him I had permanently lost the ability to believe I had a right to some happiness, and so would never get around to pursuing it. Could I ever achieve the right balance of caring, but not too much? Of supporting, but not too much? How do I sign off my children and on to me? I wanted to run away—home, back East, where I grew up. I whimpered this to my friend Hannah. She reminded me where she and I were both living now, as far as it might be from where we were born, *was* where we finally grew up, or at least were given the opportunity to.

Hannah suggested I consider doing a Native American sweat as a way of consoling myself, of grounding. She reminded me that a Lakota Sioux elder and wise man lived in Bend. He felt his calling was to share the traditions of his people, to encourage non-Indians to follow the Red Path to the knowledge of Great Spirit, or, at least, better understand the Native American view of things. I looked forward to the ceremony as a cleansing, a deep meditation, a forced separation from the chatter of the day to day, nothing more.

The sweat lodge was set up on the outskirts of Bend, out where the desert takes over, where our preoccupation with our daily endeavors start to look fleeting and silly next to the relentless gaze of land meeting sky. The structure was made of layers of tarps and cloth secured to ribs of willows bent into an igloo shape. The path to the entrance was marked by two parallel rows of small, round gray stones outlining the path to the doorway, secluded under rubbery flaps of blue plastic tarpaulin. Prior to going in, each of us sat cross-legged on the ground outside among a cluster of sage, tufts of bunch grass forming a cushion under us. We spoke little as we tied tobacco pouches of the same colors signifying the same things as those left at Chief Joseph's marker in the Bear Paws: black representing the west, for strength and guidance; red, the north, for healing; yellow, the east, for introspection; white, the south, for love, compassion. We tied blue for Father Sky and all winged creatures, green for Mother Earth, and purple for the all-encompassing infinite spirit. I followed the example of the others there, carefully placing a pinch of tobacco in each small square of colored cloth, then praying for that particular strength or presence to be in my life, Sophie's, Isabelle's, Nick's, and Stephen's. I then twisted the top of the cloth and tied it to a string, a necklace of multicolored amulets. A fire, symbolic of love, had been built the night before outside the lodge and large lava rocks heated in it. The heat of the stones, I was told, was the means of bringing love into the sweat lodge. They were red hot now, hot enough to be glass, to form the clear black obsidian that Indians in this desert used to make arrowheads a century before—sharp, precise, surgical to separate flesh from pelt, snag steelhead and trout, spear the heart of the mule ear, cut clean and deep. A large bucket of water was carried in the lodge and placed at the fire tender's seat next to the sweat leader. We entered silently according to the path of the rising of the sun, approaching along the walkway outlined by the small stones leading into the womb-shaped lodge, the matrix, the center, and squatted inside. Before sealing the entrance with the tarp and enveloping us in total darkness, the leader explained what each round signified, and how they would be conducted, with more hot rocks and water added at the start of each. In the first round seven stones are placed in the fire and calling songs are chanted to call in the spirits and ancestors. During the second round, the prayer round, more stones are added and each person prays, concluding their prayer with a Sioux injunction: "homitakuye oyasin" or "all my relations." The third round, the hottest, the hardest, is the suffering round, and signifies the willingness of those participating in the sweat to suffer so others will not suffer. It is also a forgiveness round, for self-redemption. The Native belief is that dedicated suffering is sublime and painless. In the fourth round the door is opened to let in some cool air, the pipe is passed, and then the doors are closed again. The final round is filled with songs and chants to send the spirits home again, to thank and release them.

The elder presiding over the ritual was a huge man. Shirtless, he sat cross-legged as he explained the rounds to us, his long graying black hair, twisted into a pony tail, lay across his shoulder like a piece of discarded rope, like a dead thing. His naked belly hung over his waist and rested on his thighs. His small, brown eyes, even when open, were nearly covered by his eyelids. His face was pocked. His chest bore numerous small scars striated in quick, short strokes over his pectoral muscles, scars of honor, testimony he had completed the four requisite Sun Dances to become a Sundancer. At least four times he had pierced himself with cherry wood connected by a long cord to a central pole festooned with banners of colorful prayer flags, sacrificing flesh and blood for his people. He, along with the other candidates, marked the slow, deliberate, circular dance for four days, ringing a tiny bell at every step. At the end of the fourth day, they pulled loose from the pole, ripping themselves free.

This massive man spoke to us softly, gently about what we were about to do together. He talked about the sweat lodge being the equivalent of a church, only in the Native tradition the spiritual is accessed through the body. "The darkness, the total darkness in the lodge allows us to become one. Dualism is transcended. We move into oneness, all-ness." And then after a long silence: "We are ready to begin." The fire tender disappeared out the doorway and returned with the first of seven rocks. The doorway was shut by pulling down the many layers of flaps. Not a trace of light entered. Two large ladles of water were poured over the rocks and the steam began to build. There were ten of us inside, although with the intense, humid heat, and the total darkness I quickly ceased to be aware of anyone, anything. I shed my clothing and let the sweat pour off my arms, my nipples, my forehead. No one could see me and I could see no one, could not make out one detail of my hand before my face. I lost my bearings, felt suspended in space. I listened to the drumming and chanting through round one, offered my prayers in round two, as I fingered the tobacco pouches suspended on a string near my head from one of the ribs of the lodge roof. One woman prayed for fertility, another for her son to return safely from the military service. A man asked for guidance on his spiritual path. I asked to come to, to myself, to a sense of self, to be a mediator and advocate for my children. I asked for safety and protection for all of us and for the courage to rise whole above the hard things. My prayers were added to the moist, hot, primordial mixture of others that swirled inside the lodge. We exchanged breath and prayer. We lost ourselves to the space, the darkness. We honed the edges of our supplications, shaped them into tools to love by, to live by, sharp and precise. The third round was excruciating for me—the most rocks, the most steam, the most exacting, the most purifying. Some murmured prayers. Others moaned and collapsed onto the damp ground to escape the heat that rose and nested inside the cervix of the lodge.

After the fourth and final round, I pulled my clothes around me and followed the others who crawled out into the night on hands and knees. I encountered hardly a night, hardly a darkness, compared to where I had been.

And where was that? I had eventually gotten over feeling trapped thanks to the fire tender who told us, as we sat and dripped with sweat, that the lodge was a symbol of infinity, the universe, of all things. "Let yourselves go into that space, and do not be afraid. This darkness is not an enclosure, but a vast and limitless space. Everything is like this—can constrict or free, depending on how you look at it." When he said that I remembered, like a familiar smell or taste, something I had once known: this is where we are to live each day—in trust, in faith, in love, even when you can't see. I didn't call Debby at her apartment. I didn't call Debby's parents in Minnesota. I held Sophie as someone who would of course be all right. I acted in faith that she would call me. And she did.

"Did I ever tell you, Mam, about when I was at Trek West for that Christmas? We were in the Cascades, walking through snow up to our waist. It was freezing. I thought my toes were going to fall off. We made camp for Christmas Eve. We used sausage skins tied together to decorate a tree near our tents. The only Christmas treat we got from the staff was a handful of Hershey Kisses. It was the second night of our three-week trek. Hershey Kisses in bright red and gold tinfoil wrappers. I'll never forget them. The chocolate smelled so good, tasted so good, after nothing but trail bars and rice and sausage. Everyone gobbled theirs. Everyone but me. I saved mine in my pocket. I only ate one every once in awhile. I even had one left when we came into the McKenzie for take out, when you and Stephen came to get me, three weeks later. No one could believe it."

That's probably all I need to know, isn't it? That she could endure, persevere, suffer and in the midst of it meter out pleasure, reinforcing her ability to save, to plan, to anticipate. If there is anything to emotional IQ, Sophie was off the charts. We were learning to free ourselves, despite the darkness, thanks to the darkness.

FIFTEEN

When Waves Move Words

After my divorce, the children and I had more than once gone to the same small town on the Baja Peninsula and rented a ramshackle, barnlike house made of adobe brick. My cousin and her husband owned it. From the first time we went, the town felt familiar to us, we instantly felt at home. The Mexico expressed by this town was giddy and joyful, its people seeming to grip harder on happiness the more they suffered, the more they were without. This simple Baja culture wove play and color and music into the day in proportion to hardship. I wanted to do that. The sun rose in the morning and the people's spirits with it. Amidst the chatter and clatter, they were jovial in the face of the absurdity and the injustices of life.

So here we were, again, the summer after Sophie successfully completed her junior year. We had that to celebrate. But also Stephen's and my engagement and the completion of a small house we had built there. The idea was to go, all of us, still in pursuit of that ephemeral thing called family, and celebrate our engagement, christen the house.

I was feeling pretty shaky about saying yes to Stephen. I couldn't separate him from my past experience, wondered if I ever could.

When we got there, each of the children staked immediate claim to their order in the peck: Isabelle took charge, Nick abdicated and then resented being discounted, Sophie hung around the edges. Stephen clamored for a branch on the tree, but none had yet been assigned to him. And I danced back and forth between saying what I felt and saying what I thought everyone wanted to hear. Familiar roles for each of us. How to be together differently, to learn different ways of being together? Learning to stop, look, and listen to each other, to allow for the possibility that change had taken place, that we were different now. Isabelle's boyfriend, Erik, came too; they had by now "morphed" as one of their friends described it, having dated for seven years.

Stephen had arrived ahead of us to finish up some things, including the casita, a Mexican version of a bunkhouse for the children to stay in. We arrived and that first evening Erik gestured me aside and asked if he could talk to me. "I want your permission to ask for your daughter's hand in marriage," he said. I responded with tears—the same ones shed at weddings and funerals, weeping about the too much I know, about the truths revealed when held up against others' lives. I hugged him and said yes, yes! I could feel his heart beating fast in his chest. "I'm going to write it in sea shells and white stones underwater when we go snorkeling tomorrow, but wanted to tell you ahead of time," he stated earnestly. I hugged him again.

The next morning, with our old van stuffed with towels and snorkels, coolers of drinks and food, and two kayaks, we drove to our sandy destination. The sea was rougher than anticipated, but the day sunny and hot. We set up our individual encampments on the white sand—towels, sun lotion, books—and headed for the water looking like beached sea monsters, our brows squished into unusual expressions from the tight masks, the snorkel sticking up from our heads, walking in our flippers like ungainly lemmings, determined to make it to the sea. Sophie, Isabelle, and I swam together, gradually working up our confidence as we got used to the ocean-bottom sights— colorful schools of tiny fish, sea anemones in full bloom on the rock faces. Suddenly Isabelle started swimming as fast as she could toward shore, screaming through her snorkel tube, the sound like someone calling from inside a subterranean cave. Sophie and I followed flippering madly, not looking back. Certainly she had seen something that would devour us all in moments. We got to the beach breathless. She was crying in pain. Up and down her arm were red welts from a species of jelly fish that, it appeared, was in season. "I will not go into the water again," she pronounced after regaining her composure and rejecting the various suggested remedies for the sting, which included all of us peeing on her arm. She saw no humor in it. Erik immediately told Isabelle that he needed some time alone, which she took to mean he was upset with her, that she wasn't a good sport, that he expected her to go back in the water after being stung, and that he was insensitive if that was what he thought. Sophie and Nick, meanwhile, had snuck off to drink beers and when they got back, clearly in a party mood, asked if they could use one of the kayaks. Stephen got them launched and before long they were headed around a rocky outcropping, out of view. I let Stephen know in no uncertain terms my opinion of him letting them go on a kayak when they had been drinking. Just then Erik reappeared, although out of Isabelle's view, looking nervous and frustrated. He gestured emphatically to Stephen to please come help him. I was growing increasingly concerned about Sophie and Nick and no sooner had Stephen begun trying to help Erik gather small white rocks, than I called him back to go find Sophie and Nick. He abandoned Erik to his underwater writing efforts and launched in the remaining kayak, soon returning with them, herding Nick back in one kayak and pulling Sophie behind his, she kicking with her flippers. Suddenly she started screaming out in pain, grabbing her arms and legs. Struggling wildly to climb into Stephen's small kayak, she toppled him into the water where he too was stung by the swarm of jellyfish Sophie had encountered. We got everyone to shore, but Erik had yet to get Isabelle's attention, as she was so riveted by Nick and Sophie's dilemma. Finally he got her to walk down the beach with him to see what he had, in defeat, written on the beach itself with shells. "Will you marry me?"

He looked relieved, although a bit bewildered, as they walked back to join us. The question asked and answered. That much done.

When I inquired what became of his plan to write his marriage proposal underwater he said: "I tried, but the waves kept moving my words." I knew what he meant, *how waves keep moving words*, plans, hopes. His hopes for his new bride, the interjection of natural forces. Seductions, conquests, sea monsters, heroes, and heroines.

Stephen and I too had signed on for a concept, launched an idea—us to be together, committed to one another. Stephen said he didn't want to marry again if it wasn't going to work. I told him he had better not then, as there were no guarantees. I wish I didn't know that so well, but I did. I knew about the waves moving the words. I hoped Sophie, all of them, would take note of our courage to commit to the possibility of happiness despite knowing the potential for fallout. For disappointment. Even for trauma. And I felt like Penelope unraveling and now knitting another version. Fay had said: "Unraveling can mean the sweater is coming undone, yes, and can feel like a bad thing is happening, an out of control thing. But the yarn is still there, right? The same amount, the same raw material—and it is possible to reconfigure it into something that is a truer reflection of each of you, of the family you can be."

This family, my family, sat and toasted Erik and Isabelle under a palapa on a terrace in front of an empty hotel in the middle of a sandy nowhere. I looked at the faces of my children. Isabelle and Erik, in some ways already married—to the idea that having a plan provided them with a guaranteed life ring. Nick, still willing to fly blind—paddle around the point in rough waters in a small kayak, destination unknown. Make a plan when he gets there, if then. And Sophie—letting someone else's lack of plan still pull her along, her tendency to assume that action equaled plan.

We arrived back at our house on the Baja that night sandy and tired and changed. The waves had indeed moved our words, what we tell ourselves and each other, slightly shifted all of us, our relationship to one another. Young and old, committing and recommitting to the possibility ("The triumph of hope over experience," as Stephen kept repeating, as if to reassure himself), Erik and Isabelle promising themselves to each other in ways they could only imagine. And Nick and Sophie now, perforce, shifted in their position, their rank, their role, nudged by the actions and decisions of me and Stephen, Erik and Isabelle, closer to their own adulthood, closer to defining and acting on their own commitments to themselves. Sophie would celebrate her eighteenth birthday in four weeks. She would be a legal adult, moved out of range of my legal control.

That summer in Bend she was employed as a nanny for a family of five children and as many horses and cars and houses. She was responsible in her work, but remained steadfast in her allegiance to Megan and Rachel, and inconsistent in her ability to walk the line. I recalled a cowboy we had on the ranch who, in frustration with a bunch of cattle that would not stay on the trail as we herded them to water, looked back over his shoulder at me, his straw cowboy hat pushed back from his brow, his arm bracing him against the haunch of his tired horse, and exclaimed: "This is the zig zaggingest damn bunch of cattle I ever did see." Sophie was headed to water, but her zigs and zags were cause for concern. I repeated Fay's advice to myself: "Hold her as able, hold her as able."

My present to Sophie on her birthday was a visit from Fay and Rory. Before they arrived I agonized I had made a mistake. I hadn't. Sophie eagerly took Fay around to meet Megan and Rachel, to her former high school, to her father's, although he stayed locked inside the house, refusing to come out. We celebrated on that summer night sitting around a table in the back yard toasting a young woman come of age. She had elected to return to Montana again to finish her senior year. She was looking forward to applying to colleges. She took a deep breath, blew out the candles, and dove deep to write on the floor of the ocean, working against the power of the tides.

SIXTEEN

Essay Question

I got the prize for coming the farthest for parent conferences, or so Sophie's teachers told me each time I made the trek. I'd check in at the front office. The secretary immediately drew the conclusion that because I was only vaguely familiar to her, and she didn't know the current status of immediate and extended family, as she did about everyone else coming in for conferences, I must be one of the Northern Lights parents. The school sat at the very center of the diadem of the tiny community, straddling a slight rise in the prairie. The rest of the town fanned out around it. The building was constructed of yellow brick, two stories high with sixteen-foot ceilings. It was built in the 1950s, featuring solid, thick wooden banisters, large squares of olive green linoleum tile on the floor buffed and polished for the occasion of the conferences. Six or seven lockers flanked the walls outside of each classroom, in contrast to the armies of lockers that filled a space the size of a football field at the high school in Bend. The walls were decorated with samples of the students' art or writing, instead of posters admonishing kids against drugs, reminding students what behaviors to report and to whom, that otherwise might result in dangerous and aggressive behavior. Sophie had remarked how cool it was that nobody stole anything in Bow, that everyone could leave their lockers unlocked, that all the posters on the walls of the high school weren't about the possibility of something negative happening—drugs, pregnancy, STDs; that no school "resource officer" walked the halls with a pistol in his holster as they did in Bend. Bend, Oregon, like other up-and-coming, picket-fenced, SUV-ed, and latte-ed boomtowns across the country, was armed and at the ready to defend itself against the new enemy—its own children.

The secretary leafed through her files, sneaking a look at me from time to time over the elaborate frames of her glasses, no doubt wondering what it would take to send her child so far away and for so long. She found Sophie's report card along with the schedule of conferences and took the liberty of studying the sheet, reading Sophie's grades, before I had a chance. "Oh, yep. Just as I thought. Northern Lights." She looked up at me again. "Well, Mom, looks like she's holding her own. Glad to have her here."

"Thank you," I replied, checking my irritation, reminding myself that everyone in this town felt they had certain privileges when it came to information about anyone else. It was why Fay, when I challenged her about allowing Sophie to test the waters and go to parties in Bow during this, her senior year, had said everyone knew everyone and made it their business to keep track of where the kids were. The households holding the parties assumed each teenager would bring a sleeping bag along, the unwritten rule being that if there was any alcohol at all, they would sleep on the floor, instead of taking any chances driving the long dirt roads home late at night.

If this school's hallways did display inspirational posters they could have boasted how this community looked out for its kids: hands-on, nosy, straightforward, realistic. A good night's sleep followed by eggs and bacon, biscuits and gravy. I recalled the beleaguered personnel at the Bend high school, one of three in town, designed to accommodate 900, now bursting with 1,500 students. Hallways were body to body during class changes. Students were often quickly mislabeled as either good students or trouble makers—the latter indicated by absences, truancy, missing homework. The school counselors didn't have time to ferret out the whys and wherefores of these symptoms of deeper issues. It was all they could do to plow through the maze of record keeping, attendance sheets and interim reports. By then a student might have missed two weeks or more of school. Before I took offense at the secretary's inquisitiveness, I recognized she cared, took interest, that Sophie's success was important to her. "Gonna join us for the game too?" "Yes," I answered. It was the homecoming dance weekend and one of the reasons I had wanted to come, in addition to the conferences. I wanted to see Sophie in the dress she bought for the homecoming dance, "black with feathers decorating the neck" was how she excitedly described it on the phone. She had gone with friends to Billings to pick it out. Tiny Bow High School was in the football playoffs this year despite barely managing to field a full team, never mind substitute players.

I wasn't sure where to look for Sophie. She knew I planned to go straight to the school. She said she would find me there. I headed for the first conference on my schedule, and lined up in the hallway with other parents, fathers in coveralls or faded denims, the cuffs pooling at the top of their scuffed cowboy boots, standing next to their wives who wore jeans and colorful shirts with mother-of-pearl snaps. There was no way to tell who was the more successful by their dress or manner. No one established their pecking order by external plumage, I thought to myself as we eyed each other. None said hello, but neither did they stop their conversations, as if I were a chill wind from the outside. They kept right on talking and unofficially included me, as though I would know exactly who Nedalyn was and that she had gone to Billings for the week to take care of her mother and why her husband, George, had decided to turn his cattle out early and what kind of new barley seed their neighbor Earl was going to try out. What *could* they have said? I might as well have had Northern Lights brand on my forehead. How's your daughter? No, that would imply something was wrong. Glad to be here? Well, yes . . . well, not exactly—I mean in a perfect world none of this would have been necessary. So they did the next best thing, catching me up in their stories, like a rogue tuft of airborne yarn. I realized how different I looked. I wore jeans, but my shoes were not useful for much. My coat was a long one, camel hair color. They were probably thanking their lucky stars they didn't live off in a city somewhere, where kids while away their time on skateboards—no chores, nothing to tie them to the earth at all, to a sense of being needed or necessary. I wanted to tell them that had been my plan, and more: I could rope or brand with the best of them, make soap from pig lard, ride a full day, use a calf puller and mother-up orphans. That I, like them, wanted a place where my children could fold into the undulating hues of living on the land. But waiting in that hallway, I guess they couldn't know.

I had recently driven out into the High Desert to the ranch where I had lived with my husband, taking a writer friend from Bend with me. I wanted to hear what words the place prompted in him—the deep cut of the valley, the way the house squatted down in it, the corrals that spawned out from the one side of the barn, the South Fork that serpented through lush hay meadows. It had been a long time since I had been there. I drove us by the hired man's house where various families lived while we ranched, like the newlyweds from Oklahoma. She starched and pressed her husband's dungarees, hanging them on the line from wire stretchers. He always wore leather work gloves to keep his hands from getting chafed. They found the going too rough, packed up and left. Or Darcy, who rode an unruly, dapple-gray stud horse, and her diminutive husband whom, the rumor was, she regularly beat up. And George and Doreen, who daily wondered out loud why the good Lord just didn't finish off the whole thing, the world had gone so bad. The hired man who lived there now looked up from what he was doing, called off his dogs as they challenged the tires of my car. He squinted at me like I was from outer space—just as I would have upon seeing a woman driving in the desert in an old Volvo station wagon. "What in the Sam Hill?" he probably muttered. He went inside, maybe to call the main place, where we were headed, alerting them to this unusual sighting. "But," I wanted to roll down the window and shout, "this is my ranch. I conceived all my children here. I know where the water holes are, where the gates are, where the draws are that will help funnel the cattle down off Tiger Butte. Can't you see that?

Don't the thin lines that fan out from my eyes speak of riding alone across Silvies Flat during the winter, in snowy stillness, a herd of curious antelope running back and forth in front of me, like dolphins playing off the bow of a ship? What about the way my hand falls off a point midair by the breathtaking memory of a desert lily in early spring, pushing through the rocky, dry soil?" Looking at the woman driving that car, standing in that hallway waiting her turn for teacher conferences, none of you could tell?

I was called into the English teacher's room. She greeted me matter-of-factly and turned to Sophie's page in her grade book. Just then Sophie came hurtling in, a friend in tow, and gave me a boisterous hug. "Mam. You're here! I am so excited! I have to go to the gym and finish decorating for the dance—but I'll come find you in a little bit, OK?"

I nodded yes and turned back to her teacher. She smiled at me. She went on to extol Sophie's writing skills, her inquisitiveness, her desire to ask, to know, to challenge. Her records plainly charted when Sophie's attention would fall away and then return. "Overall, she's very bright, doing fine." She then pulled a sheet of paper from Sophie's folder. "This is the start of her college essay. I gave it as an assignment. Depending on her plans, she'll need to complete this and any applications by Christmas and get them in. You might want to talk to her about it. It's a good start. Very honest. Very brave." She returned the paper to the folder. I looked at the teacher and wondered what she knew, what the essay said.

I checked into room 205 in the Bow Motor Inn. The room had come to feel like my own. I had given up staying at Northern Lights to give Sophie and me a chance to be alone together, so she could enjoy the opportunity to be in town, have a bathroom to herself, a TV (there was none at Northern Lights). Her date for homecoming was a solid, strapping ranch kid, and her very good friend. As was the tradition, when a Northern Lights girl was doing something special, all the other girls came to cheer her on, be it a speech competition, a play, a choir performance, or high school dances. So when Sophie was readying for her date that night, all six of the other girls plus Fay squeezed into room 205 to offer advice on the color of eye shadow, Sophie's hair-do. And when the knock was heard at the door, the young cowboy's expression of disbelief at the transformation Sophie had wrought was there for all eight of us to see and tease him about. "You fix up pretty good," her escort stated breathlessly. He didn't do so badly himself, dressed in a rented black tuxedo with a green cumberbund and a black cowboy hat. The awkward exchange of corsage and boutonnière accomplished, the two walked down the narrow motel hallway, her arm in his. Outside, he opened the door to his pickup and, with flourish, gave Sophie a hand in.

I asked Sophie to show me her essay—what she had done so far. I was curious, after her teacher's comment. I encouraged her to fill it with details of all she had done, to speak up about what she had achieved, to boast. How else would the colleges know? Like every parent ever, I wanted for Sophie what I had had—only better. I wanted colleges to know how wonderful she is, to want her. At that stage in my life I was utterly unaware of myself or anything else. Sophie, her brother, and her sister had different things to write about in their college essays than I had. I pictured Sophie walking along a sidewalk that crisscrosses a college campus somewhere, in the winter, self-important brick buildings surrounding the quadrangle, she all bundled up, off to have coffee with friends, feeling safe, secure, and good about herself. I wanted her to feel that way. Isabelle had completed college, but with only one toe in the water, seeming to not quite believe she deserved the fun of campus life, taking refuge in her relationship with Erik, experiencing life through him. Nick watched as his friends entered their first, then second year of college and still it was not something he could make room for in his thinking. I laughed at myself as I replayed my fantasies for my children to attend private secondary schools, except now the goal was college. As Fay said: "It's OK to have fantasies—just don't act on them."

After I returned to Bend, I faxed Sophie a copy of her resume she used to get a job the summer before, again urging her to incorporate some of her past accomplishments in her college essay. She called to tell me how surprised she was to see herself as the person this resume described. The life it described sounded so on track, like it had a shape, a charted course, a direction. Could that be her? She assured me she would weave some of it into the body of the essay she had written. A few weeks later she faxed me her final draft.

My Life in Focus

As my hand gently adjusts the lens, the world moves into focus. My finger depresses the shutter and a feeling of satisfaction inundates me as I watch the sun slowly sink out of the frame of my camera. I got the shot.

Maybe my recent interest in photography stems from my desire to bring my life into focus. There had been things—my father's drugs, my mother's struggles as a single parent, my brother's and sister's methods for dealing with what had hurt them, and my own tries to keep the truth about certain events in my life out of focus.

What I have realized is it's not possible to keep certain things out of focus without everything else getting out of focus. By avoiding the negative things about my family, I lost my self, my sense of direction, and my family.

I temporarily lost the picture of my childhood that I cherish, the experience of growing up on a ranch and developing a relationship with animals. My mother's worries about money and the personal challenges of raising a family left me and my brother and sister to pretty much raise ourselves.

I didn't value my promise as a student who completed a yearlong research project as a high school freshman on the effect of lawn fertilizer on an urban marshland. I didn't focus on my achievements as an athlete who played varsity and JV soccer as a freshman, who qualified for Nordic Junior Nationals in freestyle and classic competition, who was recruited as a competitive swimmer, who is an accomplished Western and English horsewoman, hiker, and snowboarder and certified in outdoor leadership and wilderness skills. And since there is no letter awarded for many of the "sports" I engaged in—wrestling calves at a branding, moving cattle on horseback, driving swathers and tractors, irrigating acres of land—I felt they didn't count.

I didn't see clearly my abilities as a pianist selected to play at three State Honors Piano recitals, the State Syllabus competition and Bach festival; or as an artist whose mask, made from a file folder, bark and straw, was selected for the PTA exhibit at the Oregon state capitol. My pottery and sculpture won overall in the regional art competition my senior year in high school. My watercolor of a geisha was auctioned locally in support of a local family resource center for $200. I neglected to see the accomplishment of my collection of poems, and photographs that now grow along with my ability to keep things in focus.

In the past I failed to focus on what these attributes said about me. I also chose not to appreciate the honor and recognition bestowed on me by adults and my peers when chosen as a representative in the Natural Helpers Program, a peer counseling workshop; or my selection as legislative page in the Oregon House of Representatives.

I overlooked my years in 4-H experience winning a first place in swine showmanship and livestock judging. I chose not to see that the traveling I have done—to Hawaii, to New England where all my relatives live, to Canada by sail boat, to the San Juan Islands to camp for three different summers—enriched my view of the world. Or that two years of Spanish plus trips to Mexico have resulted in a solid start at Spanish as my second language.

I overlooked the community service I have done including working at the HIV Hospice shelter during my freshman year, at the senior assisted living center as a junior, and the volunteer highway beautification program my senior year.

And why was so much out of focus? Because I was not willing to see that I had a personal fight to fight against my drug use during my sophomore year. It blurred my view of my self and my life. I could only see being forced to participate in a wilderness therapy program, and then being sent to Montana for a year of high school. But it was there I found a family and a ranch and rural community that brought me and my life back into focus.

And now that I begin to see myself clearly, I ask you to do the same. My academic record may not, at first glance, look flowery and accomplished, but look again. Despite the turmoil of my sophomore year, I am a solid student. My athletic skills may not seem varsity quality, but look again at the variety of athletic skills. My community service record may not seem impressive, but look again and you will see someone who met high school requirements while working 30 hours per week. I know what it is to work, to study, to give, to love, to hurt.

I have the camera in my hands, and I bring the world into focus. My finger depresses the shutter. A feeling of satisfaction washes over me as I watch the young woman move out of the frame and on into her day, her future. I got the shot.

SEVENTEEN

Playing with Mirrors

My father had a habit of giving me mirrors as presents. Perhaps he unconsciously thought these mirrors would help me to see myself truly, to consider what showed up in my life might be a reflection of me. Two in particular are my favorites. One is a Mexican mirror framed in tin, cut in the shape of a flower. The dulled end of a nail in the chestnut hands of an unknown pointillist artist indented fleur-de-lis and snail-like shapes in the thin, gray foil around the looking glass. When I look into this mirror my face is wreathed by an elaborate headdress, a tin halo, an aspiring angel. The other mirror is small, oval, and hangs from a tiny chain in my bathroom. Embedded in the mirror itself are tiny pressed flowers, squashed flat but forever displaying their original brilliant colors. My face is intersected by their beauty, a floral tattoo superimposed on my chin, eyebrow, or cheek, depending on my angle of reflection.

Passion clouds vision. In my passion for the West, I didn't see it for what it is and isn't. In my passion for the marriage and life I wanted to believe I had, I clung to a distorted view. In my passion for my three children, am I capable of ever seeing them clearly? These fun houses filled with mirrors that distort our perspective should not be where we live, as I did, but only where we go to be reminded of our ability to be fooled.

At a summer day camp when Isabelle was eight, a fellow camper told her not to look into a mirror at night because the devil would look back out at her, his eyes glowing red. I don't know what effect that had on her, but when she told me, it scared me. To this day I don't dare look in a mirror at night for fear I will encounter the red-eyed devil. This is the stare-down my children and I have to win. We were preyed upon by a man who became irretrievably preoccupied with his distorted image of the world and sought to insist it on those closest to him. In the company of a demented narcissist, we became prisoners of the image he painted of and for us, of the red-eyed devil looking out from the mirror at night. And because it is the familiar (in this case familial) image, in order to survive we tolerated, even imitated it. My task was to shatter the mirror that held my children spellbound, the mirror their father held up to them. My job, I felt, was to jolt us out of the trauma trance we were all in, free this band of Patty Hearsts who had become sympathizers with their captor.

There were and still are times when I feel his dark side is winning, times when it seems no matter what I do, the red glow reflecting off his presence in our lives colors our nights and days. Fay says the goal is to first acknowledge that feeling and then step outside of it, claim yourself. "Dispel the shadow. It is not you. The bad things that happen to us are not us. If a battle is fought on a movie screen, the screen remains intact. If a cloud passes over we are not fundamentally changed because of it. Cross over to the sunny side of the street." That's what Fay says.

My mother used to wake up in the morning, stand by her bedroom window that looked out over the rolling hills of western Massachusetts, scratch her buttocks through her peach-colored satin nightgown and sing: "Oh what a beautiful morning, oh what a beautiful day." I now believe she sang to chase away clouds of doubt, regret, uncertainty, weariness. She actively established, first thing in the morning, that the day for her would be a sunny one. She might as well have chorused: "Let me be a magnet for good things." Someone once described my life as a magnet for suffering. It shocked me. All the self-help books coached that it is important to take such phrases and turn them into a positive affirmation. "Please do not let me be a magnet for suffering" becomes "Let me be a magnet for good things." If there is any truth to our ability to feed negative or positive outcomes, it is worth making these small semantic adjustments. As Wayne Dyer preaches: "You'll see it when you believe it." What you in fact believe deep down is what you manifest in your life. Can it be? Days were I thought maybe the simplest thing would be to stay inside, not cast my light or shadow or any aspect of my personal energy out into the world for fear of what I might unwittingly attract. What kind of magnet was I?

My last summer on the ranch I took a trip out into the Steens Mountains, where a land-locked lake attracts an amazing array of rare birds—pelicans, egrets, whooping cranes. A vast valley floor houses this lake, which expands and contracts to the same unplumbed and mysterious rhythm as the Great Salt Lakes—due, probably, to some powerful injunction from the moon. This valley is the former home of massive volcanic activity. One diversion is to hunt for lava core bombs or, as I call them, singing rocks. They have passed through fire and ice twice, essentially. The first eruption rocketed them into the atmosphere as a glob of hot lava. They tumbled down, cooled and came to rest as a small rock. The next eruption, hundreds of years later, threw the same rock back into the boiling cauldron, only this time recoated with new, red hot molten lava, elevated to such an extreme temperature that the original core fractured into tiny fragments, trapped inside the more recent outer core that had cooled and solidified. The insides were slivers of glass that, when the rock was rattled, tinkled and chimed like a miniature chandelier. I hunted the desert floor for these brown rocks, roughly the size of a grapefruit. I scoured the vast Harney Lake bed, picking up any round possibility and shaking it hard next to my ear, looking like a mad woman for whom the winds and dryness and sparse living of the desert had sent her over the top. It might have been true. I came away with three singing rocks, one for each of my children, with spangled, whispery wishes sealed inside, fragile glass hopes encased by fire, trauma, cold, and isolation.

I know about holding songs and secrets inside, the damage it does, because I did it for so long trying to hold a marriage together with a man, I now realize, who was not only suffering from drug addictions but also was mentally ill. I lived with my own secrets about the abuse I experienced, convinced no one would listen, believe, or care. And too, the feeling of being alone with these monumental secrets, and my belief that I had no one to turn to or trust, often sealed me in silence. I also kept my secrets in order to preserve some piece of the life I felt was promised to me. I was determined to salvage something of my fantasy of how I wanted things to turn out. The fantasy had become me, mother and rancher. I believed I had nothing to replace it with. I believed I'd vanish, would go into total freefall were I to tell myself and others the truth about my situation. What I know now, having climbed out of the hole I was in, is keeping secrets, convincing others to keep secrets, maintaining facades to protect us from our own truth, prevents us from healing, distorts our sense of our own reality. Whatever the secret is, it should be told. As soon as it is, it loses its power, becomes a story, even a song. If we protect the enemy, individually or as a family, we can not heal, can't help others heal.

The secrets we keep stake their claim, keep part of us hostage, prevent that part of us from being in life, in love. Once the boulder is rolled away from the entrance to the cave, light can shine in. Resurrection truly takes place. Our children's task is to survive their parents, but they have to know all they can about them in order to survive them. It is about claiming a right to life. If we don't as parents tell our truth, and if, as Fay says, "children express what we suppress" . . . fill in the blank. We reap what we don't sow.

The singing rocks reminded me of the secrets and songs inside each of us, buried beneath layers of molten life, waiting to be freed, to be heard. Rock hounds and collectors who prowl the High Desert for lava core bombs take them home and split open these coconut-sized treasures, like a prehistoric aepyornis egg, to find inside crystalline caves, light refracted into tiny rainbows by minute stalagmites and stalactites, a miniature heaven.

One of the last things my father said to me before he died was: "Don't live your life backward." I am surprised he didn't give me a rearview mirror. What did he mean by that? I turned the phrase over and over in my mind. Did he mean it literally? At first I assumed so, for I had shared with him my questions about whether to return to live in the East, what affect it might have on the children, what work I could find, where would I live? I took his statement to mean not to move, as I would be retracing my steps, going backward. But then I thought maybe the act of standing still, staying in the same place, clinging to a life that had randomly landed me in Bend, Oregon, was living my life backward out of caution and fear. Maybe he meant not to live out of regret or guilt over past actions, not to let my coat tails get perpetually snagged on a nail in the past as I try to move forward. Like the "not going back" rule that Fay coached—not rerunning old tapes, not reliving the same set of feelings of upset and guilt over and over again.

Whatever he meant, I have concluded that the trajectory of our life force or energy, if tangled and snarled, is reflected in our life day to day. If it is a lance of translucent light thrown with intention at a target, the universe pays attention. Not that it necessarily delivers that target, but it pays attention. It is not a life of stasis. Translucence—the antidote for the red eyes in the mirror is to overflow with light.

Night driving, that's what it's like writing about something as our lives continue to unfold around it. The night swallows up the portion of the road we just drove over, while the head lights illuminate the highway ahead. A dear friend back East admonished that I should keep my lights on low beam as I dealt with all that was going on, so I wouldn't see too much of what stretched before me and be overwhelmed. Maybe so, but I feel we have an obligation to vigorously embrace the stories we are given in life. We must feel along the ridges and crevasses of the story until we get to know it and recognize our responsibility to it before it is too late, before it tells us. So I offer this telling to parents, single mothers, families combating addiction, families keeping secrets, people struggling with shame or guilt—with the hope that maybe this act of disclosure will help illuminate the road ahead, help put a stop to lives lived backward.

It goes like this:

Though all of us in our family of five were severely affected by drugs in one way or another, I have chosen to tell the story of my youngest child. Why hers? I begin to understand why now as I tell it. This is the story of finding a way to help my daughter right herself. Where and how. The choices. Getting real and letting go. This is the story of a father's addictions, and how they moved stealthily through all of us, ripping out pages of our family's album of hopes and our supposed rights to happier times. Of extraordinary courage and extraordinary fear. It is a story of miracles born of hardship. Of not giving up. Of gracelessness and blessedness. It is also the story of reckoning with my drugs of choice. Shame, guilt, fear, denial. Like any drug, they distort reality, make meaningful exchange impossible, and dangerously slow reaction time. In bearing witness to my daughter's emergence, I was able to author my own.

EIGHTEEN

Highest, Best Use

After a long day spent cooking for twenty, moving cattle horseback, I used to love to lie on my back on the grass in the evening, after putting the children to bed, and listen to the sounds of animals settling in. Our lawn was separated from the irrigated hay meadows and the desert beyond by a split-rail fence that W-ed its way around our irregularly shaped yard. I looked up into the giant black tarpaulin, tiny punctures of light growing brighter and brighter as the sun gave up its hold. I was at once made to feel bigger and smaller by the vastness—earth and sky—equally unfathomable, and, from my vantage point lying on the grass, equally as unpeopled. The Milky Way hovered soupy over the sleeping sage hills. The call of the coyote marked the parameters of encroaching darkness. My meditation might be interrupted by the distant growl of a low flying aircraft moving stealthily across the velvet dark, but nothing more.

This High Desert suited me, my propensity to gaze and ponder, analyze and think, to be still. Ranch life complemented my inclination to fall into line with the dictates of nature, harvest, and birth repeated over and over again. It was a life that rewarded caring, adventure, courage. It required humor, patience, and humility. Some say the High Desert is an acquired taste: gnarled, windy, dry, and sparse. Oregon's Outback. Maybe so, but I am certain I can claim to have walked where no one has walked before, been the first to discover a teepee ring of stones circling the campsite of nomadic Paiute tribes cycling through a century ago, or initials carved in the bark of a juniper marking the passing of a hapless covered wagon looking for the promised land.

It wasn't here. The High Desert isn't the promised land—sending many homesteaders away discouraged that nothing would grow, bedeviled by the wind, the cold, the dust—as much as it is a land of promise. For me the promise included the chance to put myself in perspective, in relief against the backdrop of an unobstructed view, relative to the big picture, the big plan, the big sky, the big land. It included the privilege of living life out, away. When I was first married and moved to the ranch I remember how crippled I felt: there was no one to call to come over, to visit with, nothing to do—no one but myself to fall back on. But I countered by learning about and taking comfort from land and animals, and by resurrecting skills and talents I'd forgotten I had. I took the promise offered by the landscape seriously, laid my life on the line for it, left my homeland for it, staked my family and my soul on it with complete faith that if I did my part it would do its part. It would deliver a life well-lived—honest, vigorous, wholesome.

I remember nights I would drive home from town with a month's supplies: groceries to stash in our walk-in cooler, the size of a New York studio apartment, along with cattle vaccines, tractor parts. It was nothing to cover 250 miles, hit two or three different towns in search of what we needed. At dusk I'd head home, fifty miles on the highway before making the turn-off. Once off the highway, I'd speed the car over the rough, dirt road, the tires kicking up rocks. I knew every curve, every rut. The night would close in over me like a quilt. The stars hovered motionless over my speed, making mockery off my sense of going somewhere. The flat, dimly lit landscape played the same game, any forward progress only noted relative to the shadowy form of a juniper tree along the road that would flash by. The smell of the sage wafted into the open window. I rested my elbow on the window frame, drove with one hand. The silhouette of Tiger Butte told me I was halfway home. Once in awhile the lights of a ranch house would peek around a cluster of poplars or willows. Once in awhile a coyote would dart in front of me. I hastened home to my husband and children, eager to hug my happiness in close. I used to tell the children a Native American fable that says each time a story is told it makes a hole in the night sky, adding a new star. One of those stars I saw above me, pretty and bright, was ours, our story, our blessed life, I was sure.

Probably because of the same perceived sense of promise, wilderness therapy programs have sprung up all over the West, taking kids into the out-of-doors to find themselves, to take nourishment from all that big landscape seems to offer. Wilderness as therapy. The notion that land can fix a kid. It sells. It sells on the back of tightly held beliefs and fantasies about the West, "where a man's a man and sacks are made of burlap," where people are solid, strong, truthful, honest. The idea sells big in Montana, Idaho, Oregon, and California, with over 100 programs opened since 1990. In Oregon alone there are thirty. Bend is the home base for six. The Oregon legislature has wrestled with how to evaluate and regulate these programs, which cater to kids who have lost their grip and sense of place and are thrown at the rugged outdoors to discover it and themselves again. There has been fallout. Two ran off from a program and held up an elderly ranch couple. At a residential program near the Three Sisters Mountains, the school's director molested the girls who attended. In another, a staff member tried to subdue a belligerent young man who was threatening to do harm to himself and in the process the boy suffocated. But considering the numbers of kids moving through these programs and the condition these young users are in when they arrive, the statistics are good overall. The turnarounds are happening. The desert is delivering, reminding these young men and women that they are part of a bigger plan and are glorified in it, that there is a container big enough for them and their dreams. The question is how long can they remember what the desert tells them? How long will a restored sense of self keep the rain out?

I don't see myself as a victim so much anymore. Bad things happened to me and my children. So OK, I will move on, and am moving on. But I do feel something has been taken from me. It's more than the moments I thought were my God-given right, more than the fact that I feel robbed of an intact family, a husband who is the father of my children, and a lifestyle—hay to swath, chickens to feed. More than that. I am scared I am unable to relearn how to be in the world, to bond, to keep on keeping the rain out. For all intents and purposes I am fine. If you met me you'd think so. But I wonder if I can ever trust, have faith, attach to someone in a healthy way? The fault lines where my fractured heart is knitting together are fragile. They get resevered by the slightest thing. I see it in my relationship with Stephen. I see it in my inordinate hopefulness over the smallest sign of good news in the children's progress—and then my utter desolation when it doesn't turn out. Black and white are the only colors in the spectrum of possibilities. I see it in my assumption that people don't want to know me. Daily, I have to talk myself out of that. Make myself go into the swirl of the public. Every day. To earn a living. To live a learning.

And too, my view of these once embracing spaces has been changed, tainted. I can't hold the desert the same way. I now see child abuse lurking behind the tidy stacks of hay, the addiction behind the drinking at the grange hall dances, behind the pain medications. I now see wives coerced into having sex in the isolated bedrooms miles from nowhere. I now see the children molested by their fathers behind the red barn, while cows graze in the meadow, swishing flies with their tails. And when I hear the ranch life extolled as the only way to raise a fine, strapping, honest, hardworking kid anymore, I want to break the news—it isn't necessarily so. Not all the stars in the night sky mark the telling of happy stories. Not all of the lights are stars.

Though I didn't know it at the time, while lying there on the grass in our yard, gazing at the heavens, the low flying aircraft I heard was likely as not the county sheriff with ultraviolet cameras scanning the range to pick up the heat generated from the night burning methamphetamine labs that hide out in the desert, or to hunt for signs of marijuana farms and their grow lights. What I didn't know at the time was drugs would claim my husband, turn our family upside down.

Invert the desert's night sky and you will have constellations of a different sort. The meth cookers stand outside, regardless of the temperature, smoking nervously, jittery from their meth use, not daring to go inside with a lit cigarette—might just as well throw it into a bucket of gasoline. Setting up in the isolated areas near ranch and farm communities in Washington, Oregon, Colorado, California gives the producers access to the one chemical they need most: anhydrous ammonia contained in farm fertilizer. Rural hardware stores have lots of acetone, Coleman fuel, charcoal lighter fluid, and the other ingredients used to manufacture this drug. In the rural areas, bored young farm and ranch kids are being recruited to sell the meth or to take it.

Sophie told me she could buy drugs on the school bus on her way to middle school. Eighth graders in rural America are 104 percent more likely to use amphetamines, including meth, than their urban counterparts. Oregon is one of the nation's top producers of the stimulant. More than 230 meth labs were seized in Oregon in 2000 with reports still being filed. The young high school girls in Bend use meth to stay thin. The boys use it to feel big. A recent bill before the Oregon legislature proposed that children found in meth-using or -producing households be removed. The presence of the drug was placed on the same level as child abuse. The neglect children of meth users experience is as devastating as their exposure to the toxic and corrosive chemicals used in the production of the drug. For every pound of meth produced, there are five and six pounds of highly toxic waste. These children are living in houses that turn the moisture in their lungs to hydrochloric acid.

Bend, Oregon—another Western boomtown that claims to be in the heart of God's country—is located on Highway 97, identified as a drug corridor from Mexico, through California, and on to Canada. The county recently was given the auspicious honor of additional federal monies because it was designated as a drug hot spot, due primarily to meth use. Ironic isn't it, the vans loaded with kids on the first week of their three-week rehabilitation likely cross a dirt road that leads farther out to a secluded lab? I can picture the meth cookers and pot growers tracking the vans with their binoculars to make sure there is no chance of being found out, as they stumble unwittingly over old tepee rings, snag their shirts on a juniper tree emblazoned with a pioneer's initials. When asked how often social service agencies in central Oregon come across a case that involves meth, the answer is every single day.

Most of Oregon's High Desert belongs to the Bureau of Land Management (BLM) or the Forest Service; land the homesteaders didn't want the government took back over. Up until recently, ranchers leased back rights to graze their cattle on BLM or Forest Service ground. Many ranches were bought and sold on the strength and size of their government lease. The BLM used the quaint and now outdated measure of "animal units" to calculate how many acres of their public land it would take to carry a cow for one year. In the High Desert it was higher than on almost any other area of public lands. There isn't much for a cow to eat, nevertheless cattle grazing was, for years, considered the "highest, best use" of this vast, arid, rocky territory. *Highest, best use* is the term the BLM uses in evaluating what they permit on their public lands. Now it seems the process has been contaminated by the sullen vagaries of our social appetites. Now the warring highest, best uses are drug production and drug rehab. Is this as good as it gets?

I have always relied on the desert for answers. Maybe the answer isn't to be found there anymore. Maybe our instinct to self-destruct is going to overwhelm even the best possible promises, the best possible uses, the best possible places. The underbelly of my West turned up white, powdery white. Will there be anything left of the wide open? Was there really ever a place discouraging words were not said?

NINETEEN

Best of Show

When we first got Sophie's 4-H pig, we had been off the ranch for seven years. We had been involved with 4-H before moving into town. Isabelle had excelled in it, the pants, zippered jacket, and duffel bag she sewed qualifying her for the state finals. Nick, as one of the Snapshooters, had brought home blue ribbons and every year managed to snag or tackle a chicken or a pig in the chases staged by 4-H leaders. 4-H was well organized and a wholesome summer activity for rural children—whether they raised an animal, learned leather tooling, cooked, or painted. So though we were living in town, I made arrangements for Sophie to join a club outside the city limits and got permission for her to participate in their county fair. I can't recall any logical thought process that led us to the conclusion that raising a pig to show and auction was the thing to do. Something about Sophie wanting to earn money for school clothes.

After work one day, I picked up Sophie and we headed for a ranch that had piglets advertised for sale. I pulled my Volvo into the dirt driveway. I was still in my tailored pant suit and high-heeled boots. Sophie and I looked over the litter, not fooling anyone, least of all ourselves, that we knew what to look for, finally pointing at a pink one with brown spots. We watched, impressed, as the rancher deftly snagged the piglet's two hind legs and stuck the squealing captive head first into a burlap sack. He looked at me, hesitated, and then handed the sack to a startled Sophie, who managed to wrestle the squirming bag into the back of my small station wagon while I wrote the amused vendor a check. Sophie climbed in the back trying to contain the frantic piglet—who was squealing and wriggling and, yes, defecating through the weave of the sack all over the car.

The pig was to live at a friend's who had some acreage. We had earlier constructed a pen and it was with relief that we got the piglet situated with water, fresh straw for bedding, and the rations recommended by the 4-H manual. Twice a week every day that summer leading up to the August fair, Sophie and I would drive out to see Punky Brewster, as the pig had been named. Sophie would curry, bathe, and weigh her and then go to the 4-H club meeting where, in addition to learning a lot about animal and particularly pig husbandry, she also had to maintain a log of her pig's progress. The club members practiced showmanship techniques with their pigs, training them to respond to the tap of a wooden cane on their haunch or snout to get them to stop or turn. Punky Brewster's weight was important, as a pig could be disqualified from the fair for weighing too much or too little.

Pigs are very smart, something we came to appreciate, and very humanlike. Punky adored Sophie and vice versa. Whenever Punky spotted Sophie, the delighted pig raced back and forth the length of the pen, coming to a delirious halt at Sophie's feet, waiting to be scratched behind her large, bristly ear. At first contact she rolled on to her side in a state of bliss, her mouth turned up at the corners, her tiny eyes closed to better savor the moment, grunting contentedly. Sophie's apparent understanding of the "when in Rome" theory surfaced. She soon was sporting a tight French braid in her hair, instead of long, loose locks. Switched to "ropers," as the low-heeled cowboy boots are called, in place of skater shoes. She donned tight-fitting denims in lieu of the baggy style she had previously favored. She excelled at every aspect of 4-H, conducting a workshop on papermaking for extra credit, passing her written test about pigs and rations with flying colors. Punky was gaining weight at a rate that appeared to be on line with the deadline for weigh-in, just a few short weeks away. It was when we changed Punky's rations to include more molasses, more fat for a final push to the weight limit, that it began to occur to Sophie that this was all about Punky being on someone's dinner table. Sophie wasn't as inured to the idea as the other, more veteran 4-H'ers in her club. She avoided Punky's gaze. When the day came to move to the fairgrounds for the two days of judging and showmanship before the final auction, even Punky knew something was up. She was jittery, off her feed. Sophie caringly decorated Punky's small stall in the show barn with wooden signs the club had made, Punky's name burned with miniature letter brands into the surface. We camped at the fairgrounds, and the two were together all day long. During the showmanship competition, Punky followed Sophie as dutifully as a puppy—stopping, turning at the slightest tap of Sophie's cane—as if model behavior might spare her from whatever uncertainty was ahead. Sophie was awarded Grand Champion in Swine Showmanship.

The day of the auction was the biggest day of the fair. The rides had arrived—Ferris wheels, gravity-defying spinning discs, bumper cars. Every 4-H building was bursting with displays of oversized zucchini, canned mysteries, crocheted afghans. Karaoke stages were set up and locals took their turns enthusiastically crooning their favorite tunes to an average audience of three or so. Chickens panted in tiny cages. Rabbits' pink eyes glared peevishly through the bars of their hutches.

I had just sat down in the bleachers that surrounded the auction ring when I heard Sophie's name called, announcing her as the Grand Champion of the showmanship class and then declaring Punky's weight. The auctioneer began his chant. The programs were flying up into the air, indicating bids. Charitable organizations and big business owners used the auctions as their way to do a good deed, often bidding the price per pound up so high that kids walked off with hundreds of dollars in profit. That's what was happening here. But if there had been a champion show pig under that pork bristle hair the day before, there was no sign of it today. Punky would have none of it. She hightailed it, first tearing around the ring, looking for an escape, then behind the podium, snagging the auctioneer's microphone cord as she flew by with Sophie in pursuit. After two laps, Sophie gave up and sat down in tears as Punky drew the highest price for a pig that day, offered by a philanthropic group from Portland. When the bidding ended, Sophie walked over to Punky, talking softly. She calmed Punky down by scratching behind her ear. The two walked side by side out of the arena. The next morning early, large diesel cattle trucks pulled up. Armed with electric cattle prods, the drivers roughly herded the bellowing steers and squealing pigs into the belly of the semi. The 4-H-ers watched if they could. If not they turned away, covered their ears as the truck pulled out, headed for the slaughter house. Sophie was handed a check for $900.00.

They say this is a learning experience for ranch kids. Life beginning and ending is all around them. Seed and harvest, nurture and slaughter, hopes raised and dashed. Certainly Sophie was no stranger to this lesson: kittens dying from distemper, bummer lambs giving up the ghost despite our best efforts to nurse them along, beheading chickens. She knew what it felt like to have love tendered and withdrawn, to have someone she cared about betray her affections, to trust mistakenly. She showed no emotion watching the cattle truck pull out of the fair ground. Later she was wracked with tears. Ranchers say it's a dog eat dog world, survival of the fittest, when the going gets tough, the tough get going. I learned that in the desert. So did Sophie. But it does get better.

TWENTY

Processional

In anticipation of Sophie's graduation from Bow High School, I notified my sister and brothers on the East Coast, Sophie's two aunts on her father's side, and their father in Vermont, the only living grandparent. Whenever there was a significant event taking place for any of my children I tried to rally the family's attention—for Isabelle's twenty-first birthday, for Nick's high school graduation, in hopes they would acknowledge this passage, help give my children a sense of being part of a bigger family constellation. I also did it to provide a means of reminding my children that on all sides of them are fine people, despite some distorted limbs on the proverbial tree.

Mine was not the first divorce in the family. All but one of my siblings divorced. I have a recently married cousin who worries that his birth mother's genes, her depressions and fits of anxiety, will take him by surprise, that he is doomed, despite the stabilizing influence of his father and stepmother. I recognize addiction or depression can be genetically predisposed, as can blond hair, thin ankles, stubby fingers, and beak noses. I know some maintain that after a certain point, the neural pathways in the brain undergo a permanent genetic change, locking an addict in the grid of craving. But I will not subscribe to the notion that it is genetically written. I hold these children as *impacted* but not *infected*, not the pawns of some preestablished condition. I am not clear anyone really knows how long, after stamping on the tail of the DNA dinosaur, it takes for this or that signal to make it all the way to the brain of the beast, to actually show up in someone. Does it happen in a single generation as the direct result of a father's or mother's genes, or does it take a decade or more? The danger of languishing in the genetic hammock is it encourages passivity, encourages those with parents who are addicted or mentally unstable to think they are destined, to use it as a crutch, an excuse for their behavior. I also know this: if all the obvious bad actors were overlooked, lopped off our collective family trees, and we looked at who remained after the pruning, there would still be plenty of opportunity in that mix for any one of us to be absolutely outstanding or utterly flawed. Go figure.

I called around to the relatives, as though they lived within a few blocks of us, as though they could whip up a lemon meringue pie and bring it along, as though they could stop by for an iced tea, didn't need reminding because my life and the lives of my children were on their minds anyway, as though we spoke often and intimately about our children, were a close-knit family, as though my former husband's sisters had come and witnessed their failing brother, supported us through it. Sophie, at my urging, followed up with formal invitations announcing the graduation printed on heavy linen stock, written garishly in the Bow High School colors of orange and black and, in raised, gold type the class of 2000 motto: "Reach for the stars." My neighbor commented it might as well have been designed by Liberace. My niece and her young family from Bozeman let Sophie know they would come, a gesture that meant a lot to Sophie. Other acknowledgments arrived from friends and well-wishers on either coast, each of which Sophie excitedly described to me over the phone. Her sense of context, of big family, big picture, was temporarily expanded and confirmed. Surprisingly, Sophie's aunt, her father's sister, who lived in Billings, Montana, replied that she and her husband would drive their motor home over for the graduation. This would be their first visit or contact since Sophie arrived in their home state two and one half years before.

Stephen, Isabelle, and I had made our reservations early to get a good fare. Isabelle left her graduate school studies and the damp cubicles of Eugene, Oregon, to come. I had offered to help Nick with his ticket if he made his plans by a certain date. He didn't. I left him to do it on his own, resisting the incredible urge to do it for him, realizing it might mean he missed Sophie's graduation.

I wasn't in Bow for Sophie's senior prom held the week before, but I had pictures. The dress—pink, chiffon, Barbie-esque. Sophie's beautiful fair skin and blond hair being fussed over by the Northern Lights entourage. Her escort—one of Bow's favorite sons who favored Sophie, wearing the requisite tuxedo and cowboy hat. It was Sophie's coming out party, coming-of-age party. The decorations featured a huge lasso in silver looping around a deep blue "The Class of 2000." Miniature silver cowboy boots with flowers in them decorated the tables that circled the dance floor. Silver and blue confetti was scattered around the sole of the boots and curled strands of blue and silver ribbon fanned out from underneath to complete the elaborate centerpieces. The music was provided by a disc jockey who juggled tunes and quips like a trick roper jumping through the whirling coils. I heard about the well-timed surprise of Sophie pulling down and off her multilayered floor-length chiffon skirt once the music started to reveal tight white jeans underneath, jauntily offset by her high shiny mules that caught the light as she danced and danced. She handed her date the skirt, which he slid down over his head. The effect, from all reports, was clever, funny, and outrageous. This girl knew how to have fun—as proclaimed by the yearbook, which titled her "most party hardy." It hurt her feelings deeply. She didn't want that to be what she was remembered for, felt there were other things. But she had, it seemed, earned it and continued to do so. I don't know who it bothered more.

When I was Sophie's age, a senior graduating from boarding school, I was being put through the tight paces of white Anglo-Saxon Protestant New England culture. I was a debutante. In those days, one was only eligible and invited to participate in the debutante cotillion if their family was registered socially, like a pedigreed animal in the Kennel Club handbook, manifested in the form of a hard-bound black directory with *The Boston Social Register* inscribed in red ink on the cover. Inside was an alphabetical listing of each family, their children, where everyone attended school, and the address of their dilatory domicile, or summer house. In fact, the *Dilatory Domiciles* was a separate publication available during the summer months. The *Social Register* was used as a phone book. The regular telephone book was only consulted if a tradesperson were needed—such as a plumber, a carpenter. You can be assured they weren't in the Register. Families were only in the *Social Register* if they were old, established, "de race"—the closest thing to tracking blood lines the northeast could claim. In any case, thanks to my mother's Boston upbringing, and my father being from an even older, Oxford-educated English family, we were, by God, in the register and therefore, on the evening following my graduation from boarding school, I was presented at the Boston Cotillion by my father along with 100 other "debs." We were being paraded before others like us—grandparents, aunts, uncles, parents, their sons and daughters. We all wore white, symbolic of our virginity and purity. Amazing there weren't little vials of our virginal urine placed on the Ritz Carlton's linen-covered tables, among the elaborate hors d'oeuvres, the silver buckets of soft drinks and juices for the young men and women, the full declension of alcohol assortment for the adults. Amazing snippets of our hair weren't collected and offered at a primitive altar set up beneath the Baroque, gold-leafed columns at either end of the massive ballroom decorated with Raphaelesque ceiling murals of plump puttis flying around. Mostly I remember my father being very perturbed that he forgot his gloves, for the dress for the men was exceedingly formal: cutaways, dress shirts, white gloves. He was a perfectionist when it came to matters of public appearance at occasions like this. Some of the fathers wore top hats. My dress was nondescript compared to what the other girls wore, so both he and I felt self-conscious as we stood in the line, waiting to be called. And when we were, my father promenaded me down the length of the ballroom, thereby presenting me to Boston society as a well-educated, well brought-up, cultured, traveled, and available young woman. No doubt those who had already paraded past with their daughters consulted with the other parents about who it was coming along now, what they did for a living (code for income level), who their grandfather was (code for ranking in overall lineage), where they summered (code for chic or bohemian or not really worth mentioning). My husband-to-be-wasn't among the young men who attended that night, though his sisters had participated in the same ritual a few years before, his family qualifying as among Boston's finest and oldest. But for those of us who did, the next month was taken up by incredibly lavish coming-out parties—twenty-piece dance bands, four-course meals, armies of waiters, huge baskets of flowers, giant tents that heaved slightly in the summer breezes coming in shore at Beverly Farms, at Essex, along Cape Cod or that drooped beneath the humid, still inland air of Connecticut. I fox-trotted and waltzed and jitter bugged, enjoyed the attention of the eager young men, their kisses boldly placed on the inside of my neck as we danced; the knee-buckling possibilities our tight, eager bodies suggested as we pressed ourselves against one another during the slow tunes.

But I had been West by this time, working one summer on a dude ranch near Big Horn, Wyoming. I had seen myself etched in the cliff faces, pasteled in the grasses. I pressed my dreams, eager and ready, into this landscape. I was in love. With my father I crossed the vast ballroom at the Ritz Carlton, confirming that the blood that coursed through my veins was an acceptable shade of blue. If the young men lined up along the walls wanted me, they'd have to cross the continental divide. I was to go West. I just wasn't yet sure how.

In addition to the prom, another significant social event held the final week of Sophie's version of "coming out" was a large branding. Stephen, Isabelle, and I arrived a day before Sophie's graduation in order to participate. Four different ranches all fielded a crew and migrated from one batch of penned cattle to another, efficiently separating off the calves, branding them, and then turning them back out to be reunited with their frantic mothers. Groups of cowboys had ridden out before dawn to gather the different bunches of cows and calves owned by each of the sprawling ranches. We would cover a territory of about 100 square miles before we were done. As part of the crew, we joined the long, slow-moving line of pickup trucks, fifteen of them, stretched out across the treeless plains, like a camel caravan across the desert. We were seemingly headed nowhere. Nothing I could discern could qualify as a landmark. But for the ranchers, the slightest rise in the land, the draw that opens to the south, the weathered ribs of a line shack, oriented them like sailors navigating by the stars. Sure enough, a set of corrals would materialize out of nowhere, the riders already dismounted, their horses staked out, and the cattle penned.

Sophie jumped right in to help sort off the calves. Soon ropes, hot irons, needles, and sharp jackknives were flying. Severed testicles sloshed about in a bucket of bloody water, to be fried and eaten later as Rocky Mountain oysters. Hoots and hollers, dirt and dust. The day was perfect. The brands clean. Isabelle and Sophie successfully teamed up to flank calves together. The rider would drag the roped calf toward them. Releasing the rope from the calf's hind feet, Sophie grabbed the calf around his belly and flipped him, using her knees and thighs as a lever, on to his side on the ground. Then Isabelle got hold of the two hind legs, her booted foot pressing against the calf's rump while she pulled the kicking legs tight and still. Sophie bent his front leg and pressed her knee into his neck. They held the calf motionless for the injections, the castration. In one instance, when it came time for the iron, Isabelle lost her grip and was kicked straight up into the air. All the cowboys applauded the ride. She smiled, a young woman reunited with a long-lost love. She had almost forgotten how at home she felt in that smoke and tumble. Once the bunch was branded, the crew opened the gate so the calves could return to their frantic mothers lined up around the makeshift corral. The cowboys urged the stunned and wobbly calves toward the cows, slapping their leather chaps, clucking and whistling and hissing their special cacophony to aid in the reunion. Then, like a circus packing up and heading to the next town on the circuit, the branding irons, vials of medicine, syringes, knives, propane tanks, coolers of sodas and beer, buckets of testicles were loaded into the pickups and the caravan set out again across the plain to the next set of corrals where the cowboys were, once again, waiting with a new batch.

Three hundred calves later, the sun colorfully protesting the end of day along the straight-edge horizon, the branding was done. Out came the beers. Time for some horseplay now that work was over. A young cowboy who fancied Sophie took the opportunity to try to flank her to the ground in a mock branding motion—she putting up a fight, not falling for just anyone. I hoped that would be the case. Still standing, covered with dirt and dust, her ponytail in a tangle, she eyed the young man and, with a twinkle in her eye, said: "Sorry about your luck, cowboy."

Nick got himself to Bow very late that night, having flown stand-by and then hitched a ride from Great Falls. I was thankful he had made it safely, impressed he had taken the initiative. My niece and her family had also arrived. After a long and lively dinner with nine of us at the table, Sophie, with Nick in tow, headed out to yet another pregraduation party. The rest of us went to bed. As I accustomed myself once again to the mattress in Room 205 of the Bow Motor Inn, I wondered what Sophie's tomorrow would bring, what she would be imagining for herself as she walked off the far end of the long expanse of the Bow High School gym floor.

Sophie and Nick had stayed out late. She had to be at the school gym by 9:00 A.M. for class and individual photographs. She was showing the accumulative effects of a week's worth of celebrating. "Point is to see how she rides this one out, if she can check herself," Fay commented. "The thought of moving on from here is no doubt pretty scary for her." I couldn't disguise my disappointment in her condition that morning. Sophie's response was to avoid contact. Nevertheless, I followed her to the gym with my camera while she put on her robe and cap. There was an air of excitement and anticipation among most of her classmates. I saw none of that in Sophie.

Fay was probably right. Sophie was scared. Maybe she saw nothing at all off the edge of the horizon, maybe she didn't see her face etched in any cliff wall, pasteled in prairie grasses anywhere.

With the photo session over and feeling increasingly like an uninvited guest, I went outside to join the others who were lounging on the lawn by the school waiting for things to get underway. Fay arrived with the entourage of girls, as well as Ron, Rory, and Phyllis—all utterly beside themselves with excitement for Sophie. Their glee was as specific to the occasion as the brands placed on the hides of the calves the day before. Isabelle was the first to spot the large motor home as it pulled up and parked across the street, guessing correctly it was her aunt. We walked over to welcome her, although my greeting was most definitely on the cool side. I simply didn't understand why she waited so long to make contact with Sophie, and I faulted her for it. Why hadn't she been a support sooner to her or to me? Where was the concern for her brother? When we create a family, we are all responsible, aren't we? Did she have some secrets about her family, some awful trauma that happened to her brother that would explain everything? A neat container tied up with a ribbon to put the problem in—I hoped such an explanation would be her graduation gift to Sophie, to all of us.

The motor home was enormous. A portion of the living area slid out of the side wall on hydraulics like a sideways elevator going nowhere. The two used the camper in their work as geologists prospecting for oil in Colorado, Wyoming, and Montana. It had all the charm of a very fancy walk-in closet—well outfitted in tightly matched tones of lavender and gray, including the hand towels. They had installed a special bed for their beagle directly behind the driver's seat. Photographs of their children and grandchildren were magneted to the small refrigerator door. Studying them I reluctantly, guiltily admitted to myself how little I knew of each of those faces, their lives and, yes, their problems. I looked over at my former husband's sister. She met my gaze. In the end we can only do what we can do. Together we rose and stepped out of the motor home onto a stair that only appeared when the door was opened.

Sophie was in the high school practicing. She was designated to lead the procession into the gym. It was orchestrated so that when each graduate entered they would walk to the door, their name would be announced and at that moment on a large screen at the opposite end of the gym, their baby picture would be projected, followed by their senior picture. They would continue walking to a large vase of iris in the middle of the room. They were to take one and present it to a parent, a loved one in the bleachers, finally taking their place in the rows of folding chairs that faced the stage.

Sophie had called me some weeks before, requesting I send an assortment of baby pictures. She had no specific requests. "Whatever you think, Mam." I sent one of her as an infant lying on a beautiful handmade quilt, wearing tiny pajamas decorated with blue rabbits and orange carrots, her eyes as bright as diamonds, every limb taut with the excitement of being alive. Another of her at two, sitting outside, the evening sunlight soft, her blond hair glowing like a halo. A third was Sophie in her first county fair appearance, twelve years before she would win big time with her pig as a fourteen-year-old 4-H champion. She was smiling broadly and displaying a large pink ribbon, awarded for her enthusiasm if not her skill at maneuvering a horse twenty times her size in a horse show for three, four, and five year olds. Sophie had listened to the judge's request to turn, go at a walk, a trot, make a circle, then full stop. Her longsuffering mount dutifully did his best to imitate what the other horses were doing, while his intrepid rider waved and smiled at the crowd, the reins dropped, hanging low around her horse's neck.

It was time to go in. We found seats in the gym along with other families. As I waited I felt old feelings of disappointment and resentment return despite my best efforts to chase them out of my thoughts—Sophie's partying, her lack of college plans, her apparent lack of appreciation that I was there. I looked over at Fay, seated a few rows over with the girls, Rory, and Phyllis. All were perched at the edge of their bleacher seats, fanning themselves with the program, quick and eager, ready for a moment they had come to celebrate fully. Not tainted by last night, nothing to do with next week, or next month. They were here right now, as solidly as Fay was present in her hugs. I got it loud and clear. "Consider the alternative," I thought to myself. "Sophie and I might never have shared this day."

Sophie launched the ceremonies, taking her position in the doorway, wearing her gown and mortarboard, head high. The processional music began. The photo she ended up choosing projected on the screen that lauded over the gym was one taken at a rodeo. She had her father's dirty work cap on, rakishly turned sideways and falling down over the brow of her three-year-old head. She was pushing his oversized sunglasses up on her tiny nose with one hand, the other gestured outward, palm toward the sky, elbow bent, as if to say: "What's the problem?" It was followed by her senior class photo taken at a studio in Havre. It showed a slim, confident girl who looked directly at the camera, shoulders turned slightly wearing black denims and a white shirt. It said confidence and then said it again. I studied the image, committed it to memory.

She made her way to the large vase of irises and reached in. Then she stopped, there, in the center of the room, as if unsure what to do next. The recorded march continued to drone over the loud speakers. There was an audible shifting of feet, fluttering of programs. She turned and looked over toward the bleachers. I waved at her, so she would know where I was, what to do. She saw me, but still didn't move, continuing to scan the crowd. Finally she started walking, but toward Fay, with the iris in hand. Of course. Who had brought her to this point? Who was absolute in her celebration of this accomplishment? Who held Sophie as who she was, only and exclusively, with no drag on her stern made of imposed ambitions and recycled disappointments? Who held only love for her while she healed, with no image of how the healing would look or when it would be done, if ever? Who allowed Sophie to right herself, and calmly helped her work through her lapses? Fay. Of course. Sophie by now had reached the first step and walked up to Fay. The girls, Phyllis, Rory, and Ron were all clapping and whistling wildly. Sophie smiled as she approached them and leaned over to hug Fay and then all the rest of them, taking all the time she needed. She then slowly descended the steps, and walked to where I sat with Stephen, Nick, Isabelle. Leaning over and embracing me she said: "I love you, Mam," and handed me the iris she held hidden behind her back.

TWENTY-ONE

Then There Was No Mountain

I was hard-pressed to give up on the notion of Sophie completing high school and heading directly to college. My goal was to try and interest Sophie in Montana State University. But graduation had folded into summer, and her ranch job at Northern Lights provided convenient distraction. She reported that she spent her days irrigating. I could see it—hip-high boots, wielding a long, narrow round of lodge pole inserted through the hem of the blue canvas, like a giant flag. She'd climb down into the water, spanning the width of the ditch with the pole end of the canvas, and then reach into the water to place rocks on the submerged end of the blue tarp to divert the flow of water out of the main ditch. Leaning on her shovel, waving mosquitoes away, she would wait patiently for the water to build up around the set, making sure the rocks held the skirt of the dam in place and that enough water power was diverted to make it all the way down the rows of alfalfa. As if second nature, she would methodically clear away small clods of dirt that obstructed the path of the glistening tendrils of water that fed the thirsty acres. I could picture it so vividly because I had done it, summer after summer on the ranch, children in tow.

When she wasn't irrigating, she would cut hay, riding in an air-conditioned swather, leaving a tidy green wake of fragrant rows of felled hay behind her for the baler to follow in a few days after the hay had cured. She would sketch long, swooping arcs in the green meadow like a skier through fresh powder, looping back over her own tracks to where she started in order to most efficiently cut the whole field with the least number of passes. In a world of her own, she would drive with her headset on and listen top volume to country and western. Another déjà vu for me. I inhaled the memories of fresh cut hay, recalled the sensation of sun's heat on my back as it shone through the window of the cab.

When she wasn't irrigating or swathing, she helped move cattle to summer pasture, calves, with their fresh brands, frolicking alongside. She helped shear sheep. She mended fences. She fell under the easy spell of taking orders, helping carry out others' plans, not forming any of her own. The last possible deadlines for the fall semester college applications came and went. I knew them by heart. Sophie didn't have them anywhere on her radar screen.

Shortly after graduation, she moved out of the main house at Northern Lights into a smaller house on the other side of the two-lane highway that intersected Fay's ranch. It was Sophie's way of proclaiming that she had not only graduated from high school, but also from Fay's program, that she was independent, on her own, an adult. She lived there alone with her new puppy. She paid rent and utilities, had her own telephone with her own recorded message, a bathroom to herself, a kitchen of her own, a bedroom. At first she took the time to nest, to haul in an old metal crate for a bedside table, to clean out the bathroom, put posters up in her bedroom, but that inclination soon gave way to neglect, to piles of clothes and dirty dishes. At night, after working in the fields, she hung out with friends—partying. She was drinking.

After Labor Day weekend, her friends broke the formation of summer and peeled off in the direction of colleges or jobs. Those who stayed behind in Bow were those with no direction, Sophie among them. I repeated my offer to her, certain the conclusion would be obvious. Help was available from me if she enrolled in college but, at eighteen, and if not in school, she would have to assume financial responsibility for herself. Once more with feeling. I said it. This was the policy I felt I should adhere to, but what if she didn't go to school and didn't take care of herself? Would I really have the strength to stick to my guns? Some weeks later, and well after the fact, I learned she had abruptly moved again, this time into Bow to, she would later explain, save on gas and rent, and to work as a waitress at the Bow Motor Inn. It was the last thing I expected.

There were reasons for concern: she avoided telling me or Fay about the move and when we finally spoke, I found her dodgy, evasive. "I'll talk about whatever you want. Don't matter." She reverted to poor English as a way of defending herself from me, of distancing herself. "I have no secrets," she defensively maintained. She had moved, she explained, into a house in Bow where her friend lived with her mother. The daughter worked with Sophie at the inn. The mother, Sophie said, had some . . . problems. The tone of Sophie's voice gave her away. It was dark, indistinct, distorted by self-deception. I called Fay to see what she knew about the situation and my fears increased with Fay's frank opinion that Sophie had put herself in an environment that no doubt felt very familiar, but for all the wrong reasons—the presence of drugs, abusive men. "She's choosing to roll in cow shit, Ellen," Fay told me, as if this was reassuring information. "She has to go there, and she has to be the one to decide when she has had enough." How long did Fay get to explain each relapse away this way? After all this heartache, time, and money invested in Sophie's recovery, shouldn't there have been real progress I could recognize, celebrate? *At this rate*, I thought, *Sophie would have been better off to slug it out at home, with me, in Bend.* "Give it up," one of my close friends admonished. "She's alive, and if not for your getting her out of Bend she might not be, the way things were going. Be happy she is alive. Some parents aren't that lucky."

Sophie was working at the motor inn restaurant the evening I arrived, so I checked in, called Fay, and invited her to join me for dinner. We chatted while Sophie served us and her other customers. She was obviously good at it, making small talk with the regulars about cattle prices, the recent rain, deftly refilling water glasses, busing tables, balancing a loaded tray over her head on her palm, placing orders. Her shapely figure was poured into tight blue jeans cinched with an elaborately decorated leather belt, causing old men to blush and young cowboys to linger. "What do they call *you*?" one inquired removing his hat in mock respect, taking in her skimpy halter top, her blond tresses carelessly pulled back and up in a perky spray of hair. I found myself feeling oddly reassured, even proud. She had, after all, landed a job. She was showing up on time, was good at what she did. "Looks like you've learned to lower your expectations," Fay quipped, only half joking.

Sophie got off at 8:00 P.M. We said good-bye to Fay, and Sophie and I walked down the street to where she was staying, two blocks away. She wanted to show me. Inside an excessive amount of potpourri did its best to offset the acrid smell of cigarette smoke. The house had two bedrooms, a kitchen/living room, and a smaller room where Sophie had flung a mattress down and had dumped her things, making no effort to settle in. She had her dog tied up to the porch rail in the small, overgrown backyard that abutted another house of similar dimension. The mother was, apparently, out of town. The daughter seemed a sweet girl and a survivor. She and Sophie knew each other before they ever said hello, recognized a fellow traveler. In all that space, within all that possibility, Sophie, like a moth to the porch light, was drawn to this young woman. I saw nothing of what I wanted for Sophie in that house so devoid of love and caring, yet there she was. I saw nothing of what I knew to be Sophie's promise. I saw everything about how Sophie saw herself. And there was nothing I could do.

Walking back to the motel, I turned to look back at the house again, one of fifteen or so tightly bunched together along the excessively wide street, a tiny house in a town so small, surrounded by an expanse so large, that it begged the question about humans' inclination to huddle. Why here, where there were so few houses they hardly blocked the wind, where you could look out to uninterrupted space down either of the two main streets in town, hear a cow bellowing after her calf in the distance and where none of the real amenities from clustering had followed—no movie theater, no shops to speak of.

The town had originally sprouted here because it was the distance the pony express could travel before changing horses—the same equine lung capacity had spawned many of the early western towns, a cadence of communities later reinforced by the advent of railroad stations and granaries, stout with wheat. Pickup trucks moseyed up and down the two main streets, their throaty diesel engines giving the impression there was some pressing work to be done, when the real mission of the trip was to see who was parked in front of the Mint Bar, who was picking up mail, who was negotiating for a new tractor at the John Deere dealership, a sure sign they had made money or had successfully landed a loan—definitely worth further investigation. Time ran in place in Bow. The only entertainment was events at the high school—assemblies, pep rallies, football and basketball games. "Go Beeters!" the only reader board in town called out. The high school mascot was a sugar beet, it too a relic of better times in Bow, when the sugar beet industry was thriving and Bow was its profitable hub. Parents regularly wore and festooned their pickups, their front yards, their daughters' hair with the orange and black school colors. The annual father–son wrestling match was one of many fund-raisers put on by Beeter Boosters. Miraculously the event had never resulted in a heart attack. Out-of-shape farmers and ranchers turned out for it and surprised themselves by fighting more ferociously than they expected to reassert their place of seniority among the men in the family. Their white bellies were shamelessly exposed as they entered the gym wearing their old wrestling briefs, vestiges of their years on the wrestling squad.

Bow overbuilt and overextended itself early on with impressive buildings made of brick or large blocks of granite, believing it was destined for the growth that instead took place elsewhere. The Bow hardware and grocery store shelves were now dusty and nearly empty, Hutterite families moved precisely and silently down the aisles in a way that seemed as out of time and place as Bow did in its pretense of being a town. The men's black beards neatly mimicked the shape of their chin, a black deacon's hat perched on their head. Their wives, flanked by wide-eyed children, trailed dutifully behind wearing ankle-length faded floral cotton skirts. Sophie was now a resident of this town. I was convinced she had overstayed Bow's usefulness to her. She seemed to have subscribed to treading water, as unsure of her relative place in the scheme of things as Bow was. I didn't consider she might not be ready to move too far away from familiar territory, might have some hard learning left to do and wanted to do it here. She knew this better than I.

The next morning we took off on a road trip to Bozeman, the home of Montana State University. I tried to coax Sophie into talking about her new living situation, about future plans, but with no success. I tried to make up for lost time, to impose my sense of values, not to mention outcome, as quickly as I could, while I had her within ear shot. The urgency in my voice was no doubt as much a giveaway as the flatness in hers had been on the phone, my preaching and coaxing as transparent a cloak over my fears as her dark voice was about hers. We migrated out of the prairie, into the vast valleys surrounded by mountain peaks that seared the sky, along wide rivers lined with cottonwood, beauty so effortless in its assembly—smooth rocks, muted colors, cattails, small islands midriver, horses catching the scent in the wind and chasing after it, tails high.

Once we got to Bozeman and were enveloped in the pell-mell of my niece's household and her two rambunctious, young children, we both started to relax. We rough-housed, painted each others' toenails, walked along the creek on their property and talked about . . . nothing much. We hung out, is what we did. I forgot about any agenda, and Sophie forgot about defending against the possibility of one. How long it had been since I let a day pass that way?

Before moving off the ranch, there were many such days, like our skating outings at the large reservoir an hour's drive away. Nick, Isabelle, and I would gather our supply of skates and, for Sophie, double runners. We'd build a small fire on the bank and skate and laugh and play crack the whip, or try holding our jackets between us to see if the wind would propel us. We'd lie on our stomachs, making half circles on the frozen surface with our blades, and peer in awed silence down through the clear ice at dark sticks and twigs and rocks

entombed deep below, as if looking into our hearts. Hawks careen-
ing off the rimrocks that surrounded the reservoir mimicked our
glee, diving and swooping. Ice fisherman peered out of their
outhouse-sized huts to watch our antics. Our skate blades traced
connecting loops, hour glasses and figure eights on the blank, glassy
canvas.

Sophie and I spent that afternoon in Bozeman making paper
doll cut-outs, folding paper in on itself under the watchful fascination of my niece's two children. We carefully angled the scissors
around the arms, legs, torso, and head, carefully cutting eyes, a
mouth, and then opening up the string of dolls that spread out across
the table linked, hand in hand. In looking at our primitive stencil I
was struck by the fact what was cut out, as much as what was left in,
makes the final design. Our losses, our gains, the empty and filled-in
spaces, what we are and aren't, make each of our stencils unique.
What fills the empty space? It is, I believe, the space faith must claim,
love must fill to cushion the tangible, to give meaning to the actual.

When we climbed into bed that night, Sophie started talking,
opening in a way she never had before. Was it being together and
away? Was it hanging out together? Was it the joy and innocence Sophie saw in her young cousins? Whatever it was, she finally trusted
enough to confide in me some of her worst fears, deepest hurts.
Likewise I confessed my terrible, lingering guilt at not getting all of
us out of Oregon right at the start.

"Why didn't I?" I appealed to the darkness, to Sophie's steady
breathing nearby. "I am so sorry."

She said nothing. We lay in the dark in silence for awhile—
letting the words settle to the bottom, watching them as they slowly
drifted down, noticing that there was nothing either one of us could
do about any of it except keep going.

"And . . . Mam?"

"What Sophie?" I replied.

"Mam, thank you, for everything. Thank you for sending me to
Northern Lights, for getting me away." She was able to say it through
the darkness, from bed to bed, like two children on a sleepover

exchanging ghost stories about ghosts whose icy grip on our hearts began to melt away when exposed to the warmth of our mutual attention, when told out loud. I was overcome with joy—about what we had shared, and that we did.

"I love you, Sophie."

"I love you too, Mam."

I turned toward the window, looking out at the night, the Bear Tooth Mountains illuminated by the full moon. *Some of this,* I thought to myself, *starts to feel not about me or any of us. Some of this starts to feel as though it is taking place in the cut-out part of the stencil, the part I can't know about, but can only have faith in. Sophie, Nick, Isabelle. Are the mountains finally getting smaller, or are we just becoming better hikers?*

TWENTY-TWO

Then There Was

As though our magical time together in Bozeman wasn't enough, I then had a message from Sophie a few days later that she had three days off from work and would be returning to Bozeman for a college tour. I was beside myself with happiness. At last the pieces were coming together. She would accept my niece's offer of their apartment, go to Montana State, get a degree and put all this behind her. On her own she was headed back to take a tour of the University! What exciting news!

The same weekend Sophie called to announce her plan to return to Bozeman, Stephen and I tackled the task of moving a five-foot-tall young Ponderosa from the back yard of the Bend house to the front, putting an apple tree in its place that would complement the one on the opposite side of a wooden bench. It was the finishing touch on an ambitious rehabilitation of the small patch of green behind my house that had replaced the 100,000 acres of ranch land I had previously called home. Stephen had nurtured so many things in our three years together, including my ability to believe I was entitled to some happiness, including my nondescript backyard. "But what if I have to sell this house?" I speculated to him when we began the project. "What a waste of effort all this will have been." I reflected on the garden at the ranch I had created—the wagon wheel gate leading into a wild sea of perennials—hollyhocks, fragrant lavender, forsythia, yellow wild roses, and trees carefully planted along the fence—all now abandoned.

"Not at all," he remarked. "We will have had the pleasure of doing it."

It occurred to me doing things for the sheer pleasure of doing them would also fall somewhere in the empty space of the stencil, and is probably where we all should try to reside on a permanent basis. Stephen continued to pause, ponder, and prune his way through the lush garden he had created where before there had been a dull square of lawn and a narrow border of dirt with a few hardy perennials that would bravely show up in the spring.

I had first gotten the Ponderosa with Sophie when she was in the second grade at an Earth Day fair, the tiny sapling then no taller than my hand. We took it home and planted it in the narrow strip of dirt that bounded the green lawn and called it Sophie's tree. It thought about being a tree for a number of years, not getting any bigger as far as I could tell. Despite its reticence, I protected it from the lawn mower by surrounding it with bricks. It was not unlike Sophie as a pensive infant, studying the world before her, like someone standing on the sidelines, swaying slightly back and forth, getting the timing down, waiting for the right moment to enter into the jump rope game, studying those already engaged in the double-Dutch singsong, or the hot pepper chant. Then suddenly, the tiny tree committed to growing. It had suddenly sprouted candles two years before and each spring since, adding inches to its height. It burst the plastic protector I had put around its narrow trunk to discourage the cats from sharpening their claws. It grew and grew. But now an action plan, an effort to make order out of chaos. It had a place in the garden design other than where it was. And too, Sophie's tree wouldn't have enough room left in its present location, Stephen explained, when it grew to full height. "Too close to the shed," he pointed out. I worried about the tree surviving the move, but saw the need for it. We dug around the tree, deeper than we needed to. Even so I worried about the fragile roots that were exposed, winced when Stephen would stand on the shovel and jump it into the dirt, for fear he would sever something critical. We reached our arms down into the deep hole, hugging the root ball, and hoisted the tree on to an old blanket we had spread on the ground. Then, standing at either end, carefully lifted the blanket, the tree teetering back and forth in the middle like an off kilter monarch, and placed it in the waiting wheelbarrow. In an unsteady processional Stephen and I lugged the tree to the front yard, where an equally deep hole was waiting—already prepared with fresh soil and fertilizer. We lowered Sophie's tree in, patting the dirt around the roots, watering and patting, watering and patting. I won't know until next spring if our effort and care sustained the tree in making such a dramatic change. That seems like a long time to have to wait.

I had left a number of messages for Sophie since our trip together, and since hearing she had gone back for a college tour. It didn't surprise me she didn't call back. Often she didn't. But at least she knew I was thinking about her. The residual warmth of our time together was still stored in my bones, like rocks in the sun.

"Call as soon as you can!" It was a message from Fay. This was unusual—this urgency, especially considering that Sophie was no longer under her supervision. As usual, Fay's line was busy. When I finally got through, Fay told me Sophie had never come back to Bow after the college tour. Fay reported Sophie had called her roommate, and, at the last minute, the restaurant to tell them she wouldn't be coming back, that is . . . one hour before she was supposed to show up for work. She apparently had taken off with two cowboys from nearby Blaine who were laying fiber optic cable between Montana and Wyoming and had offered her some money to drive one of the rigs.

Mostly I felt nothing at hearing this. I didn't feel panic or fear. I didn't imagine the worst or the best. I felt concerned but detached in a way I wasn't familiar with. Fay continued: "At this point she is driving the boat. No blaming yourself, Ellie. This is about her. I pray nothing horrible happens, like some kind of accident, so she can get to where she needs to inside herself to figure this out. What I know of both those boys is they're partyers." I agreed to let Fay know if I heard anything and hung up. I went outside with a pail of water to pour on Sophie's transplanted tree, the child of every tree before it, of every cold frost, every dry summer. I imagined the water making its way down to the roots, to nourish whatever destiny they spelled.

When do things begin? Did all this begin when I formed in the womb of a woman who didn't want more children? Did I then seek a man who would reinforce my sense of unwelcome? And did he then pass this legacy on to his children? Or did I? Or did it all begin before that? Or since then? Was it a generation back or more that the seeds of this story were sewn? Did my children's inclinations and internal dictates spawn far upstream of this life and time? When does the invisible hand that turns on a distant light first throw the switch initiating the moth's lifelong migration? Generations ago? Years ago? Weeks ago? All these beginnings, these illuminations . . . ignited every day, launching a million different odysseys.

Today Sophie is off to Wyoming, driving a lineman's rig. And tomorrow she will call and ask: "Mam, what should I do?" And I will take a breath and acknowledge that she is now the architect of her life, the creator of her own happiness and despair, and I will reply: "You should make a decision." And I will tell her I love her and she will know I mean it and I will hang up the phone and cry and have pride in what I have attempted and faith in what I will do.

THE END

Afterword

There's something I need to say about Sophie's college essay. It was her writing, but it wasn't her speaking. Not from her heart. It is hard to admit this.

Sophie did as I suggested. She included all the activities and awards and accomplishments off her resume, organized her essay around a theme. She dutifully and skillfully put it all on to the page. She endured the coaching of her Little League mother, the pressure of looming deadlines, and managed to form her thoughts into an exquisite piece of writing. She slid successfully into base, but wasn't into the game. I wanted to believe she was. I married the makings for a happy ending as evidenced by that essay. But in real time Sophie hadn't truly acknowledged her own potential, hadn't experienced regret at what she had thrown away as the result of doing drugs, each a prerequisite for the other. She was able to recite, to inscribe the lines, but they were delivered without emotion or passion, without meaning to her. It still was true—whenever she caught a glimpse of her potential it sent her into hiding. Her own light was, for her, too bright.

As for me, I had succumbed to my friends—fantasy and delusion. I, once again, was willing to persuade Sophie to override her personal truth and offer a false self, so she'd "look good," "get in," "be accepted." She did a good job of it. I forced my wish for her to internalize her potential, unrealized and unrecognized by her. I talked her into "branding" and "marketing" her experience. Her essay is masterful. It may have helped her get into college, but it further distanced her from herself, with a leg up from me. My endorsement of a false picture of a reformed and penitent daughter, so artfully rendered by Sophie in her essay, hid my guilt and shame behind a picture prettier than the real one. I got high on the happy-ending syndrome. Never did I ask her: "Does this ring true for you?" Sadly, my best codependent intentions wrapped the same old message up in new paper: You aren't enough as you are, you aren't enough unless you configure yourself like this. And I am not enough unless you do.

Relentlessly, wave after wave, the issues of addiction reveal themselves, not just in the more obvious appetite for drugs or alcohol, but, in my case, in the more complex and subtle addictive behaviors that define my days and life, and etch on the horizon the mountains I have yet to climb. When I get out of my way, the one thing I want Sophie to know is this:

> All you need to know, you know already.
> All the love you crave, is available to you now.
> All you want to be, you already are.
> And, in that place to which your best dreams
> Take you, there are those who have been
> Waiting for you.
>
> —John Culkin

Postscript

Sophie is a liberal arts major in college.

Nick majored in filmmaking and videography in college and is doing missionary work overseas.

Isabelle received her master's degree in education and is teaching.

Stephen and I get closer to that place to which our best dreams take us. The children's father gets further and further away.